A LIFE WORTH LIVING

A LIFE WORTH LIVING

Albert Camus and the Quest for Meaning

ROBERT ZARETSKY

THE BELKNAP PRESS OF
HARVARD UNIVERSITY PRESS
Cambridge, Massachusetts, and London, England

Printed in the United States of America

First Harvard University Press paperback edition, 2016
First Printing

Library of Congress Cataloging-in-Publication Data

Zaretsky, Robert, 1955–
A life worth living : Albert Camus and the quest for
meaning / Robert Zaretsky.
pages cm
Includes bibliographical references and index.
ISBN 978-0-674-72476-1 (hardcover : alk. paper)
ISBN 978-0-674-97086-1 (pbk.)
1. Camus, Albert, 1913–1960. 2. Conduct of life. I. Title.
B2430.C354Z37 2013
194—dc23
2013010473

CONTENTS

A LIFE WORTH LIVING

PROLOGUE

"Even my death will be contested. And yet what I desire most today is a quiet death, which would bring peace to those whom I love."[1]

Albert Camus' prediction, written in the last decade of his life, has been borne out, though perhaps not his hope. Over the past several years, contests have simmered and burst over the French Algerian writer's legacy.

Shortly after becoming France's president, Nicolas Sarkozy made a state visit to Algeria. The visit garnered more than the usual attention, in part because Sarkozy had come to office with a reputation as a bluntly spoken conservative who saw no reason for France to apologize for its role as a colonial power. One of the stops on his itinerary was Tipasa, a mountainous town overlooking the Mediterranean. Not only does Tipasa boast a stupendous array of Roman ruins—the graveyard of an earlier colonial enterprise—but it is also a site to which

Camus had made a series of pilgrimages during his short life.

Two of his most lyrical essays, "Nuptials at Tipasa" and "Return to Tipasa," express his deep attachment to the village. The first essay, written in 1936 when Camus was an underemployed young man with oversized ambitions, describes his experience at Tipasa in frankly erotic terms: "Everything seems futile here except the sun, our kisses, and the wild scents of the earth.... Here, I leave order and moderation to others. The great free love of nature and the sea absorbs me completely."[2]

Nearly twenty years later, now a world-renowned and self-doubting writer, Camus returns to Tipasa. As he approaches the village, he remembers a visit he had made right after the end of World War II. Events had transformed the ancient site: soldiers and barbed wire now surrounded the columns and arches where he had once posed shirtless, smiling, and surrounded by female friends. During that postwar trip, Camus' spirit also seemed imprisoned; there was, of course, the backdrop of a world that had run amok: "Empires were crumbling, men and nations were tearing at one another's throats; our mouths were dirtied." But there was, as well, a youth now lost: "On the promontory I had loved in former days, between the drenched pillars of the ruined temple, I seemed to be walking behind someone whose footsteps I could still hear on the tombstones and mosaics, but whom I would never catch up with again."[3]

But these bleak recollections give way to something much older, yet at the same time "younger than our drydocks or our debris." The abiding splendor of Tipasa, Camus discovers, stubbornly resists the modern world's insanity: "I found an ancient beauty, a young sky, and measured my good fortune as I realized at last that in the worst years of our madness the memory of this sky had never left me. It was this that in the end had saved me from despair." Algeria was by then lurching toward civil war and though Camus makes no explicit mention of the events that were already set in motion, he seems to steel himself for the future: "I have not been able to deny the light into which I have been born and yet I have not wished to reject the responsibilities of our time."[4]

Posed in front of a sparse crowd dutifully waving flags of both countries, President Sarkozy gazed at the sea while listening to a member of his entourage recite a passage from "Nuptials at Tipasa."[5] Perhaps "Return to Tipasa" was too ambiguous or too political a text. In any case, when the production ended, actors and audience returned to their cars and the presidential motorcade continued to its next stop, leaving behind the ruined temple and young sky, as impervious to political posturing as are the elusive meaning and deep beauty of Camus' essays.

Three years later, in 2010, with the approach of the fiftieth anniversary of his death, Camus was again at the heart of French politics when Sarkozy suggested that Camus' remains be moved to the Pantheon. Voices on the Left immediately assailed Sarkozy for trying to "recuperate" Camus' legacy for his own political benefit. They insisted that his remains be kept in Lourmarin, the Provençal village that he discovered soon after the war and where, with the aid of his close friend, the poet René Char, he moved a few years before his death. The Right, for whom Camus is a neoconservative *avant la lettre*, declared itself shocked by these accusations. The controversy also divided Camus' twin children: while his son Jean denounced Sarkozy's effort to turn his father into an icon of the Right, his daughter Catherine, executor of her father's literary estate, thought that Camus' "pantheonization" would crown his lifelong desire to speak for those who had no voice.[6]

While Camus' remains are still at rest in Lourmarin, the meaning and significance of his work will never be.[7] In part, this is due to his Algerian heritage. In Alix de Saint-André's novel *Papa est au Panthéon,* the government approaches the daughter of a dashing and dead writer named Berger—a thinly veiled caricature of André Malraux—whom the French president has decided to induct into the Pantheon. The motivation is, well, political. As the director of the Pantheon tells the daughter, few things are more economical than a pantheonization. "We bring out the students, bring out the Republican Guard and bring out a new stamp: and all of this costs nothing." The publicity for the government is free, automatic and overwhelming. Still, there is a caveat: "You need a good client." Some "engaged writers" are too Catholic (Charles Péguy and François Mauriac), others are too Communist (Louis Aragon and Paul Eluard); one was not enough of a resistance fighter (André Gide), while another was too much of a flake

(Marcel Proust). And Sartre? Forget it, laughs the director: he is "still always wrong." He then mentions Camus, only to note that he also fails the test because Algeria had failed him.[8]

Few writers were more conflicted over personal and national identity than Camus. He was a *pied-noir,* the moniker given to immigrants who during the nineteenth and twentieth centuries came to French Algeria from other parts of Europe, becoming citizens of a nation, France, whose language they did not speak, whose history they did not know, and whose soil they would probably never step foot on. But this seemed unimportant at the time: Algeria was considered part of France, not a foreign nation containing several million Arabs and Berbers deprived of the rights of citizenship. By the 1950s, Camus resembled his mythic hero Sisyphus, bolted not to a pillar, but instead to the tragic impasse of Algeria's resistance to a foreign occupation—a *French* occupation. For many years, Camus labored for a solution that would satisfy the imperatives of justice for both Arabs and *pieds-noirs,* risking his life in pursuit of an impossible peace. Camus failed and fell silent—a silence he maintained until his death in 1960.

While Camus the Algerian continues to divide opinion in France, there is a movement toward consensus in Algeria, where an increasing number of Algerian writers claim him as one of theirs. This has been especially true since the mid-1990s and the so-called Second Algerian War fought between the government and Islamic fundamentalists. The Algerian novelist (and member of the Académie

française) Assia Djebar has enrolled Camus in her cortege
of Algerian political martyrs. He is, she writes, one of the
"heralds of Algerian literature"—a fraternal spirit she
calls to her side in order to gaze and reflect upon together
the bloody shambles of Algeria's past.[9] Similarly, during
a recent debate in France over the insufficient number of
mosques, Abdelkader Djemaï, the author of *Camus at Oran,*
recalls that Camus marveled at the beautiful simplicity of
Arab cemeteries. During a visit to Lourmarin, Abdelkader
discovered that the "gravestone is just like those of my
own deceased family."[10]

What draws these Algerian writers to Camus is less his
particularity as an Algerian writer, than the universality
of his concerns. This is yet another reason why he continues to make us uneasy. Whether seen from Tipasa or Paris,
Camus remains the man whose life stands as witness to a
kind of desperate heroism. His fierce condemnation of
republican France's treatment of Arabs and Berbers, his
whipsaw denunciation of Vichy France's anti-Semitic legislation, his lifelong opposition to the death penalty, his
courageous effort to negotiate a civilian truce in war-torn
Algeria all reflect the acts of a man who sought to mesh
his life with his thought. He failed, at times, to do so. For
example, during the period straddling the last months of
France's occupation and first months of liberation, Camus suppressed his deeply rooted aversion to capital
punishment, not only justifying but demanding the
death penalty for those whose wartime collaboration led
to the death of Frenchmen. It speaks to Camus' moral

resilience that he eventually renounced this position, admitting publicly that he had been wrong; nevertheless, rereading his wartime articles calling for rapid and merciless justice chills one's blood.[11]

These inconsistencies remind us, of course, that Camus was all too human: an obvious point that our desperate need for heroes, especially now, often obscures. More important, perhaps, they also remind us that Camus himself was aware of these shortcomings and sought, through his acts and writings, to explain them. In the case of his wartime position on capital punishment, there is Camus' remarkable lecture, given in 1948, when he admitted he had been wrong (to be discussed in a later chapter). And it is not difficult to read his short novel *The Fall* in part as a brutally candid confession to his serial infidelities during his marriage to Francine Camus. (This, at least, is how his wife understood the book. "You owe it to me," she told her husband upon the book's successful launch.)[12]

It is this persistent uneasiness, this unhappy inability to be lulled by the rationalizations we give for our own actions or the actions of others, this accursed gift of forcing not just oneself, but those around one, to reconsider beliefs one has always taken for granted, that makes Camus so important. He had the habit, as Tony Judt wrote, to look "in the mirror of his own moral discomfort."[13] His work and life, in turn, held that same mirror up to the rest of us. At one time a true moralist, Judt suggested, defined those who "not only made others feel uneasy, but caused themselves at least equal disquiet too."[14]

A moralist is not a moralizer. The latter has the answer before he is asked the question, while the former has only questions after she hears the available answers. And it is the questions that, as the French say, *déranger*—disturb, or more literally, disarrange what has already been arranged. Camus was, in this respect, a moralist. These questions did not lead Camus to solitude and nihilism, but instead pulled him toward solidarity and a form of ethical exigency. He was a moralist who insisted that while the world is absurd and allows for no hope, we are not condemned to despair; a moralist who reminded us that, in the end, all we have is one another in an indifferent and silent world:

> I have sought only reasons to transcend our darkest nihilism. Not, I would add, through virtue, nor because of some rare elevation of the spirit, but from an instinctive fidelity to a light in which I was born, and in which for thousands of years men have learned to welcome life even in suffering.... To the unworthy but nonetheless stubborn sons of Greece who still survive in this emaciated century, the scorching heat of our history may seem unendurable, but they endure it in the last analysis because they want to understand it. In the center of our work, dark though it may be, shines an inexhaustible sun, the same sun that shouts today across the hills and plain.[15]

The experience of suffering is central to the life and work of a moralist. Certainly, this conviction girds the visceral opening of Camus' early essay *The Myth of Sisyphus:* "Judging whether or not life is worth living amounts to answering the fundamental question of philosophy."[16] For many of us—perhaps including those not yet aware they belong to this number—this remains the fundamental question. Are our lives, filled inevitably as they are with pain and loss, worth our while? The ancient Greeks, the deep source of Camus' inspiration, had no doubts: suffering had its advantages. As Camus' beloved Aeschylus has his chorus announce in the *Oresteia,* "We must suffer, suffer into truth."[17] Martha Nussbaum's remark on the educative role of suffering in Greek tragedy also applies in spades to Camus: "There is a kind of knowing that works by suffering because suffering is the appropriate acknowledgement of the way human life, in these cases, is."[18] The genius of Greek tragedy is that it refuses answers or resolutions. Instead, its value lies in its ability "to describe and see the conflict clearly and to acknowledge that there is no way out. The best the agent can do is to have his suffering, the natural expression of his goodness of character, and not to stifle these responses out of misguided optimism."[19]

This observation applies to Camus' work and his life, of course, but we must be careful. Suffering was no more an answer to the world for Camus than was the recognition of our absurd condition. As early essays such as "Nuptials at Tipasa," as well as his last work, *The First Man,* recall with ravishing power, Camus loved the world. He was uneasy with those indifferent to its beauty, blind to the sensuous allure of the landscapes of his native

Mediterranean, and faithless toward their fellow human beings. To be a moralist, as the Epicureans understood, means one must be a sensualist. It was not just the reality of his suffering, but also his rootedness in our world that allowed Camus to declare, without a hint of sentimentality, that even though "it was the depths of winter, I finally learned that, within me, there lay an invincible summer."[20]

When I wrote my first book on Camus, *Albert Camus: Elements of a Life,* I tried to situate his thought and writings in four pivotal moments to his life, seeking to explain their meanings through the contexts in which they unfolded. I believed then, and believe now as a historian, that there was much to be said for such an approach. But by the time I had completed the book, I was also dissatisfied: bound to the historical context, I felt I had slighted certain intellectual or moral themes we have long associated with Camus' work. As with absurdity, some are elements of the human condition; as with fidelity or measure, they are virtues toward which humankind must strive; or as with silence or revolt, they are both elemental and ethical facets of our lives. They are, in short, what I believe are necessary parts of our effort to define a life worth living.

I

ABSURDITY

"There is just one truly important philosophical question: suicide. To decide whether life is worth living is to answer the fundamental question of philosophy. Everything else . . . is child's play; we must first of all answer the question."[1]

Among the most celebrated challenges of the twentieth century, the opening lines to Albert Camus' *The Myth of Sisyphus* left André Malraux, the dashing novelist and intellectual, unsatisfied. As an editor at Gallimard, France's most prestigious publishing house, Malraux, who had been deeply impressed by Albert Camus' other manuscript, *The Stranger,* found the new work labored and meandering. "The beginning stumbles around a bit," he counseled the author: "Since you have made clear that the essay will adopt the perspective of suicide, it's unnecessary to repeat it so often."[2]

Malraux was wrong: the essay adopts the perspective not of suicide, but of our absurd condition. If, one day, we discover ourselves in "a universe suddenly divested of illusions and light"; if we nevertheless insist on meaning, but instead hear only "the unreasonable silence of the world"; and if we fully absorb the consequences of this silence, Camus affirms, suicide suddenly imposes itself as the sole response.[3] Malraux's stricture notwithstanding, this is why the essay's celebrated opening line still demands our attention. If the question abides, it is because it is more than a matter of historical or biographical interest. Our pursuit of meaning, and the consequences should we come up empty-handed, are matters of eternal immediacy.

When we confront the question, however, we discover that traditional philosophy fails to guide us. Philosophers have no purchase on this subject, Camus writes, which is "simultaneously so modest and so charged with emotion."[4] Perhaps for this reason, many professional philosophers have insisted, and some continue to insist, that it is a false problem, glistening dully like a stream made brackish by the confusion of formal categories or the abuse of language. Yet there are other philosophers who now criticize their guild's failure to grasp the stubborn presence of the absurd in our lives. As Robert Solomon insists, the absurd "poisons our everydayness and gives our every experience a tinge of futility. . . . We find ourselves desperately trying to move more quickly, to nowhere; or we try to 'entertain ourselves.' "[5] In terms less dramatic, but equally emphatic, Thomas Nagel compares absurdity with what he calls "the view from nowhere." This view tears us from our everyday subjective experiences and forces us to assume an external viewpoint—a perspective that rattles the conceits and assumptions we hold about our lives. This view forces upon us truths that are both prosaic and paralyzing—that we need never have lived or that the world will continue without the faintest of shudders when we die. In seeing ourselves from the outside, Nagel notes, "we find it difficult to take our lives seriously." At such moments, we confront absurdity—a "genuine problem which we cannot ignore."[6]

Hence Camus' decision to leave behind philosophy's traditional vocabulary and techniques. Rather than a chain of arguments, *The Myth of Sisyphus* is instead a salvo of impressions, some intimate, others literary, all of them urgent and lucid. The *Myth* is an essay, similar to those written by one of Camus' models, Michel de Montaigne. In its pages, Camus pursues the perennial prey of philosophy— the questions of who we are, where and whether we can find meaning, and what we can truly know about ourselves and the world—less with the intention of capturing them than continuing the chase. Camus no more worried that there remained "something provisional" to his work than Montaigne did that his self-portrait kept changing.[7] In fact, Camus achieves with the *Myth* what the philosopher Maurice Merleau-Ponty claimed for Montaigne's *Essays:* it places "a consciousness astonished at itself at the core of human existence."[8]

For Camus, however, this astonishment results from our confrontation with a world that refuses to surrender meaning. It occurs when our need for meaning shatters against the indifference, immovable and absolute, of the world. As a result, absurdity is not an autonomous state; it does not exist in the world, but is instead exhaled from the abyss that divides us from a mute world. "This world in itself is not reasonable, that is all that can be said. But what is absurd is the confrontation of this irrational and wild longing for clarity whose call echoes in the human heart. The absurd depends as much on man as on the world. For the moment it is all that links them together."[9]

Absurd reasoning, Camus warns, surges with an urgency alien to traditional philosophy: no one, he insists, has ever died for the ontological argument. Even the great explorers of the absurd, thinkers who have bent their minds to reach firm conclusions, have with few exceptions swerved at the last moment from this journey. Kierkegaard, Camus declares, blinked first in his confrontation with the lidless gaze of the absurd. The Danish thinker's "leap of faith," far from being a heroic act of lucidity and logic, amounts to philosophical suicide. Rather than leaping into a world where absurdity rules, Kierkegaard retreats to God, to whom he gives "the attributes of the absurd: unjust, incoherent, and incomprehensible."[10] Even an absurd god, Kierkegaard confesses, is preferable to an unfathomable void.

As with an earlier Christian thinker, Blaise Pascal, who was famously frightened by "the silence of these infinite spaces," Kierkegaard was terrified by the prospect of a life lived in the absurd. But Camus insists that, for the absurd man, "Seeking what is true is not seeking what is desirable."[11] But we must not cease in our exploration, Camus affirms, if only to hear more sharply the silence of the world. In effect, silence sounds out when human beings enter the equation. If "silences must make themselves heard," it is because those who can hear inevitably demand it.[12] And if the silence persists, where are we to find meaning? What must we do if meaning is not to be found? Can we live our lives without the reassurance, once provided by religion, of transcendental justifications for the world and its denizens?

The question, Camus concludes, is "to find out if it is possible to live without appeal."[13]

As a literary and philosophical quarry, the absurd first appears in Camus' journal in May 1936, the same month he defended his dissertation on the subject of neo-Platonism at the University of Algiers. "Philosophical work: Absurdity," he assigned himself as part of his study and writing plan.[14] Two years later, in June 1938, the absurd again appears on his to-do list, then a third time at the end of the same year. Though he is mostly at the stage of research and reflection, Camus had already decided to approach the subject more or less simultaneously through three different genres: as a novelist, playwright, and essayist. He had begun work on his play *Caligula* in 1938, though it was first performed only in 1945. As for *The Stranger,* Camus completed a draft just days before the Germans smashed through the Ardennes in May 1940. And it was at that same moment, when France still appeared, if not eternal, at least solid and secure, that Camus yoked himself to what he described to his former teacher Jean Grenier as his "essay on the Absurd."[15]

During this same period, Camus discovered another young and still unknown French writer who was grappling with the absurd. In 1938, the veteran journalist Pascal Pia, who had founded an independent newspaper, *Alger républicain,* had hired Camus. Given the paper's straitened financial situation, Camus quickly found he was juggling many tasks, including that of book reviewer. Two thin books by Jean-Paul Sartre soon came to his attention: *The Wall* and *Nausea*. In these remarkable works, Sartre described a world awash in pure contingency. Caught in the undertow of events for which there is no ultimate or external justification, Sartre observed, we are overcome with a sense of nausea. What other response can we feel when we discover that events, once imbued with meaning, are in fact arbitrary; that our acts, once invested with intention, are only mechanical; and that the world, once our home, is simply alien.

Still, though the stories were compelling, Camus concluded that they offered little more than a kind of existential solipsism. To be sure, the "intense and dramatic universe" informing the stories in *The Wall* was striking, but what were we to make of characters incapable of doing anything meaningful with their freedom? Similarly, in *Nausea*, Camus marveled at Sartre's depiction of the world's oppressive density, but insisted it was wrong to conclude "life is tragic because it is miserable." Instead, our tragic sense of life lies in the world's "overwhelming and beautiful" nature—without beauty, without love, and without risk "life would be almost too easy." From the heights of his youth, Camus affirmed: "To observe that life is absurd cannot be an end, but only a beginning. . . . What interests me is not this discovery [of life's absurd character], but the consequences and rules of action we must draw from it."[16]

Though young, Camus was a veteran of the absurd. When still an infant, he lost his father in the purposeless mayhem of the Battle of the Marne; as an athletic teenager, he coughed blood one day and discovered he had tuberculosis; as a reporter of *Alger républicain,* he discovered, behind the universal values of liberty and equality of the French Republic, the grim reality for the Arabs and Berbers living under the colonial administration; as the paper's editor, he inveighed against the absurdity of a world war that, as a committed pacifist, he unrealistically insisted could have been avoided; and as a pacifist exempted from the draft because of his tuberculosis, Camus nevertheless tried to enlist: "This war has not stopped being absurd, but one cannot retire from the game because the game may cost your life."[17]

He was, in a word, already fastened on the lessons to be drawn from an absurd world. He shared this conviction not just with his readers but also with his fiancée, Francine Faure. (The couple was waiting for the finalization of the divorce between Camus and Simone Hié, a glamorous and seductive woman whose drug addiction defeated Camus' efforts to cure.) Camus told Francine that most everyone thinks the war is absurd, but this amounts to little if anything at all since they then go on living the lives they had always lived. But what interested him were the ethical consequences of this insight: "What I want to draw is a humanistic way of thinking, one that is clear-sighted and modest—a certain kind of personal conduct in which life would confront life as it is and not with daydreams."[18]

Eventually, it was Camus' insistence on consequences that forced the closing of *Alger républicain* in 1940. Already hated by the local authorities because of his relentless attacks on their treatment of the Arab and Berber populations, Camus doubled down once France declared war in September 1939. Though without illusions about Hitler's Germany, a "bestial state where human dignity counted for nothing," Camus also refused to nourish illusions about the purity or lucidity of France's leaders.[19] He was convinced that the powerless—workers, peasants, small merchants, and clerks—would pay the price of this march to war just as his own father had in 1914. (He had not yet understood that the powerless, in France and the rest of the world, would nevertheless pay if the Nazis were not opposed by military means.) The censors, intent on maintaining public morale, suppressed growing chunks of the paper's front page; Camus, equally intent on outwitting the censors, would reprint passages from literary classics, such as Voltaire's entry on "war" from his *Philosophical Dictionary*, to fill the gaps. Even this, though, did not survive the officials' scissors.

In November, Camus confided to his journal: "Understand this: we can despair of the meaning of life in general, but not of the particular forms that it takes; we can despair of existence, for we have no power over it, but not of history, where the individual can do everything. It is individuals who are killing us today. Why should not individuals manage to give the world peace? We must simply begin without thinking of such grandiose aims."[20] This same credo—which not only expressed Camus' impatience with the passivity entailed by an existential worldview but also reflected his austere professional ethic—appeared at the same moment on the newspaper's front page under the headline "Our Position." Pascal Pia, the editor in chief, and Camus sought to explain to their readers why white blocks increasingly checkered the paper's dwindling number of pages. They first denounced the very existence of censorship, dismissing the "sophistry that in order to maintain the nation's morale its liberties need to be suppressed." They then affirmed the "right to defend those human truths which recoil in the face of suffering and aspire towards joy.... Men of good will refuse to despair and instead wish to maintain those values which will prevent our collective suicide."[21]

It turned out to be the editors' swan song. Less than two months later, the authorities shut down the paper and Camus was out of work.

Thanks to Pia, who had connections in Paris, Camus soon find a position in late March 1940 with the mass daily *Paris-Soir,* owned by the industrial magnate Jean Prouvost. Unhappy in the gray and grimy capital, Camus was disgusted by the paper's syrupy style. *Paris-Soir,* Camus wrote, "was rotten with sentimentality, prettiness, self-indulgence, all the sticky references which a man uses to defend himself in so harsh a town." Far better, he insisted, to confront the bleak reality obscured by these cowardly strategies—a reality underscored by life at the seedy hotel where he had rented a room. One day, a fellow resident killed herself by leaping from her third-floor window onto the courtyard. She was little more than thirty years old: "Old enough to live, and, since she had lived a little, to die . . ." It ended "with a three inch split in her forehead. Before she dies, she said: 'At last.'"[22]

Yes, at last: France, at war yet not warring, was itself ready to utter these same words by the end of March 1940. The country had been at war with Germany for more than half a year, but it was an odd kind of war—a *drôle de guerre,* of course—during which the two nations had scarcely fired a shot at one another. Children skipped to school with schoolbags strapped to their backs, tables were crowded at restaurants and cafés, nightclubs and theaters played to packed houses. While the Paris Opera was rehearsing the world premiere of Darius Milhaud's *Médée,* Parisians were humming the popular ditty *"On ira pendre notre linge sur la ligne Siegfried"* (We'll hang our washing on the Siegfried line). Meanwhile, the actor and singer Maurice Chevalier followed one hit song, *"Paris Reste Paris"* (Paris is still Paris) with another, *"Ca fait d'excellents français."* Of course, those excellent Frenchmen praised by Chevalier—bankers and bakers, Communists and conservatives, peasants and Parisians—who now seemed united against Germany had,

just months before, been at one another's throats. Opinion was divided on whether Chevalier, with his trademark
smile, was sincere or cynical.[23]

The same question hovered over the newspapers. During the winter and early spring of 1940, front pages trum-
peted the steadiness of France's political leaders, the bril-
liance of its military commanders, and the courage of is
soldiers, while the growing frequency of blank columns
reflected the determination of government censors to bury
any reports that contradicted these pronouncements. German military victories, such as its invasion of Norway during the preceding winter, were depicted as part of France's
strategic plan, while the lack of movement on the eastern
front was attributed to the forbidding presence of the
Maginot Line. Headlines suggested by the government's
newly established Ministry of Information—headlines
such as "We Shall Win Because We Are the Strongest"—
disguised the government's appalling lack of strategic
imagination and suppression of information.[24]

Suddenly, the comic absurdities of the phony war violently
gave way to absurdities of a radically different magnitude.
In mid-May, the German military command launched
a two-pronged armored offensive, one that swept west
through Holland and Belgium, the other that punched
into the Ardennes, the forest just north of the Maginot
Line that French military commanders had insisted was
impenetrable. Scarcely three days later, Panzer divisions

rolled into the northern city of Sedan, heaving south-
ward the first wave of what quickly became an unprecedented migration of human beings.

Thus began the "Exodus." As one contemporary writer
observed, "only an experience in the Bible could represent
this surge of humanity, this shifting of one part of the
country to another. It marks the return of chaos which
marked the past, the historical wilderness when the jack-
als roamed."[25] By early June, more than six million men,
women and children from Belgium, northern France,
and Paris were streaming south through France. The
word "stream" misleads, though; "congeal" more accurately describes the dense columns of civilians, joined by
an increasing number of soldiers, jostling against one
another in cars, horse-drawn carts, and bicycles. When
engines ran out of gas or tires out of air, owners abandoned their vehicles by the sides of the road, joining the
great majority of refugees condemned to flee by foot.
These great and sluggish rivers of humanity were prey
not only to strafing Stuka bombers but also to the total
collapse of civilian authority. Indeed, when the French
government, after weeks of indecision, finally decided on
June 9 to evacuate Paris, its presence had already largely
evaporated in much of the country. While the government careened from Bordeaux to Clermont-Ferrand to
Vichy, lines of communications fell apart and local representatives were left clueless and powerless. The decor of
everyday life in republican France had, quite suddenly,
collapsed.

Yet the chain of command at *Paris-Soir* remained intact. With a far greater degree of foresight and planning than the French High Command, Prouvost had weeks earlier combed the country for sites where his paper could continue to publish in case Paris was threatened. He plumped for Clermont-Ferrand, the capital of the Auvergne region in central France. Not only was the city far from the front, it was also home to the newspaper *Le Moniteur,* whose editor, Pierre Laval, agreed to share his printing presses with Prouvost. On June 11, *Paris-Soir* appeared for the last time in Paris; the remaining staff, including Camus, quickly packed their bags and joined the exodus.

By then, Parisians heard the echo of artillery fire to the north, smelled the burning of petrol reserves to the west, but could not find officials anywhere to oversee the evacuation. The void left by the government quickly filled with rumor, confusion, and fear. Assigned to drive one of *Paris-Soir*'s cars to Clermont-Ferrand, Camus headed south with a copyreader sitting beside him and an editor in the backseat. When the car finally clanked into Clermont-Ferrand the following night, the gas tank empty and smoke slithering from under the engine hood, Camus leaped from his seat, ran to the trunk, pried it open and sighed with relief: his briefcase filled with his manuscripts was still there.

The absurd, Camus observed, "is an experience that must be lived through, a point of departure, the equivalent, in existence, of Descartes' methodical doubt."[26] His novel, *The Stranger,* one of the manuscripts in his briefcase, re-creates that very experience. But Camus did not follow Descartes, who retreated to a stove-heated room in snow-bound Germany to confront the demon of skepticism. Instead, he sent his story's protagonist, Meursault, into the sun-heated streets and beaches of Algiers to confront the silence of the world.

Though many readers already know the story—after all, *The Stranger* remains, more than seventy years after its publication in 1942, one of Gallimard's best-selling books—it still unsettles our expectations.[27] In language as bare as a noonday street in Algiers, Camus creates a character whose life is empty of the shade offered by self-reflection. A lover who is incapable of love, a son unable to mourn his mother's death, and a murderer without a motive for his act, Meursault lives with no thought to ei-ther past or future, but instead glides through an endless procession of present moments. At the end of a weekend spent traveling to the nursing home where his mother had died, then making love to a woman he had met on the beach, Meursault straddles a chair on his terrace over-looking his neighborhood's main street. From noon to night, he smokes while gazing at the passersby and sky. The changing tableau gives rise to neither memories nor hopes, but instead barely rises above mere description. As night falls and the air chills, Meursault closes the windows and steps back into his room: "I glanced at the mirror and saw a corner of my table with my alcohol lamp next to some pieces of bread. It occurred to me that anyway one more Sunday was over, that Maman was buried now, that I was going back to work, and that, really, nothing had changed."[28]

With life yoked so tightly to the present that no space remains for what precedes or follows, nothing changes. Or, more accurately, it is with reflection that we see change. Moreover, it is only with change that we see reflection—our own. When Meursault glimpsed the mirror's reflection, he did not see himself—rightly so, as there is not yet a self to be seen. This is the paradox Meursault makes flesh: for him, only life lived in the moment—the moment our bodies register sensations sweeping over them—is meaningful. Yet indifferent to the past and future, he is incapable of grasping whatever meaning there is to be found. When the girl he slept with, Marie, asks if he loves her, Meursault replies that the question "doesn't mean anything, but I don't think so."[29] Nor for that matter does the Arab's death: all Meursault knows is that, upon pulling the gun's trigger on a sun-blasted day, he had shattered "the exceptional silence of a beach where I'd been happy."[30]

Of course, only a reflective being can claim he had once *been* happy. Meursault's imprisonment and trial—the fatal events hurling him into self-consciousness—resemble Jean-Jacques Rousseau's depiction of *l'homme sauvage,* or natural man, tumbling fatefully into the state of society. Like Camus, a French speaker who never felt at home in France and a man torn his entire life between the opposing pulls of solitude and solidarity, the Genevan-born Rousseau affirmed that man in his natural state was the happiest of beings because he was, quite simply, the dumbest of beings. He is a being whose "soul, agitated by nothing, is given over to the sole sentiment of its present existence without any idea of the future, however near it may be, and his projects, as limited as his views, barely extend to the end of the day."[31] Whereas prison, for Rousseau, symbolized a society that stifles our nature and shackles our needs, for Meursault prison is stone and iron. Only after he is locked in a cell does he begin to heave his life into a story, one in which he plays the leading role. Only then does he recall "a certain time of the day when I used to be happy" and does he flee what he had once, unconsciously but contentedly, experienced—namely, the interminable present, claiming that only "the words 'yesterday' and 'tomorrow' still had any meaning for me.'"[32] His earlier life was no more absurd than was Rousseau's natural man. Absurdity enters our life only when the prison door clangs shut—or when, from the heights of society we measure how far we have fallen.

Just weeks before the "Exodus," Camus had been struggling with the manuscript that would become *The Myth of Sisyphus*. He wrote to Francine from Paris, confessing his doubts over his effort to heave his notes into an essay: "I am frightened by the amount of effort and attention it requires. I am overwhelmed by my notes and perspectives." The notes grew less important as the perspectives, burnished to a blinding sheen by events, grew more important. Though Camus makes few if any explicitly historical or political references, his essay nevertheless reverberates to the cataclysm unleashed on Europe. As a result, an essay Camus first began as his own intellectual and emotional itinerary soon deepened into a quest for meaning in a world whose values and expectations had utterly imploded.

The graceless Clermont-Ferrand unexpectedly turned out to be a fitting stage for work on the essay. In a letter to a friend, Camus observed: "This city has exactly the décor of *La Nausée*."[33] A different kind of nausea, stirred not by the contingency of life, but instead by the policies of the government that had just arrived in Clermont under the aegis of the octogenarian Marshal Philippe Pétain, also overwhelmed Camus. In his letters to Francine, Camus unburdened himself: "Cowardice and senility is all they have to offer. Pro-German policies, a constitution in the style of totalitarian regimes, great fear of a revolution that will not come: all of this to truckle up to an enemy who has already pulverized us and to salvage privileges which are not threatened."[34] Looking around at political leaders and hangers-on, Camus felt as if he were suffocating. When the new regime revealed its anti-Semitic character, *Paris-Soir* fired all of its Jewish employees. Horrified, Camus told Francine any job at all in Algeria, even one on a farm, would be preferable to working at *Paris-Soir*. All too naturally, Algeria now appeared to him as the one place he could be free and still call French.

For the moment, though, Camus remained in Clermont-Ferrand. Devoting his attention to his writing, he renamed

what until then he had called his "treatise on the Absurd."
He gave it the name *The Myth of Sisyphus,* though only the
last four pages of the essay take up the myth.

Absurdity is the child of disparity. It rises before us when
our expectations fall short of reality. From the simplest
to the most complex case, writes Camus, "the magnitude
of the absurdity will be in direct ratio to the distance between the two terms of my comparison." As instances, he
suggests marriages and challenges, enmities and silences,
wars and peace treaties.[35]

Reading these lines, his close circle of friends might
think of Camus' tortured marriage to Hié and his
tuberculosis-weakened lungs, the class conflicts in Algeria he covered as a reporter and muteness of a mother he
attended to his entire life. Or they would recall Camus'
experience working at a hardware store during a summer
vacation, spending long days engaged in "work that came
from nowhere and led nowhere . . . waiting for the order
that would cause him to do some absurd hurrying about":
a rehearsal in Sisyphean absurdity. So, too, were his inevitably doomed efforts as a boy to translate silent movies quickly enough for his illiterate grandmother in order
to keep up with the reel, yet quietly enough so as not to
disturb those sitting close by.[36]

For those who did not know Camus, but did know war
and treaties, absurdity also reigned. Though there is just
one entry in Camus' notebooks dealing with the exodus,
France's experience in 1940 infuses the essay. Camus

thought this fact important enough to underscore it upon the publication, in 1955, of the American edition of The *Myth of Sisyphus*. In the preface, he asked for the indulgence and understanding of his readers. The book, he reminded them, was "written fifteen years ago, in 1940, amid the French and European disaster."[37]

France's defeat marked a violent divorce between a nation and its institutions. France's material and military resources were not markedly inferior to Germany's; in certain instances, they were in fact superior. The disparity between France's strength, measured in the quantity and quality of material, and the suddenness of its collapse, led the historian, soldier, and resistance fighter Marc Bloch to baptize the event as the "strange defeat." Had he survived the war—the Gestapo murdered him in 1944—Bloch might have agreed it was no less absurd than strange.

As for the exodus, what greater disparity could there be for the millions of refugees who, just days before they were pulled into the vortex created by the capsizing of the French Republic, still believed stupidly in the permanence of their civil, legal, and political institutions, as well as the durability of their everyday lives? "Rising streetcar, four hours in the office or factory, meal, streetcar, four hours of work, meal, sleep, and Monday Tuesday Wednesday Thursday Friday and Saturday according to the same rhythm."[38] This is the "before" of our lives, the absence of punctuation reflecting the seamlessness of our days—that is, until the moment the seams suddenly unravel.

That moment of unraveling can be as banal as an over-heard conversation or a glimpsed interaction, or as extraordinary as a Stuka bearing down on you. It is the moment when we are woken from our routine lives by a whisper or explosion, either of which demands "Why?" with equal and unexpected insistence. With a weariness tinged with amazement, staring at the empty skies for an answer or a stranger in a cockpit of a plane determined to kill us, we see the facades give way and the world "become itself again."[39] Try though we might to return to what we once knew, the strangeness of our human predicament has been restored. In all of this, our reaction is so similar to the clerk observed by Camus whose bank had transferred him to Clermont: "He tries to keep the same habits. Almost succeeds. But is just very slightly out of tune."[40]

Unmoored like so many other institutions, *Paris-Soir* again moved its offices in September from Clermont-Ferrand to Lyons, housing its staff in a hotel whose walls, adorned with paintings of nude women, reminded Camus that the building, located in the heart of the red-light district, had itself been a whorehouse. Appropriately, the newspaper had by then become a shameless promoter of the authoritarian regime now in power, faithfully echoing the reactionary, paternalist, and xenophobic claims that larded Pétain's discourses. The texts of Pétain's speeches were reinforced by photos of lines of old men and young boys—almost every male in-between was a prisoner of war in Germany—raising their arms above their beret-capped heads as they saluted the nation's new leader. When Pétain visited Lyons, the veterans of World War I filled the city's central square. Looking down on the crowd, one observer muttered that the scene reminded him of a "living ossuary."[41]

As the severity of the weather grew, so too did Camus' unease and doubts at *Paris-Soir*. When the paper announced in early October the first battery of the regime's anti-Semitic legislation, he wrote to a Jewish friend, Irène Djian, to express his disgust. "This wind cannot last," he assures her, "if each and every one of us calmly affirms that the wind smells bad."[42] He promised he would always stand by her side—a remarkable position for a Frenchman to take in 1940 when the vast majority of his compatriots either embraced or resigned themselves to the new laws. In his notebooks, he jotted down a number of historical allusions. Saint Thomas, he notes, "acknowledged that subjects have the right to revolt," while in Renaissance Siena a condottiere who had saved the city, then demanded absolute power and in return was killed by the inhabitants.[43]

Francine joined Camus in early December: the divorce with Hié had finally been registered and they could now marry. After a civil ceremony on December 3, the married couple, along with Pia and the paper's typesetters, toasted the marriage at a nearby bar. Given the lies that now passed for facts at *Paris-Soir*, Camus found solace in working alongside the typesetters: they, at least, could justifiably find pleasure in their skilled labor. For the rest of the month, when not doing the graveyard shift at the paper's offices, Camus worked on the *Myth* with Francine in his heatless apartment. Unable to find a typewriter, Camus wrote with blistered and stiffened fingers while Francine, wearing gloves, recopied the text. In that bare and glacial room, just as in this "hideous and dizzying world where even moles find reason to hope," Camus clung to his book and the world it depicted, if not for hope, at least not to despair.[44]

We know how the story of Sisyphus ends: it does not. It is a conclusion that never concludes, measured by the distance between the mountain's summit and the last stretch of slope the boulder must cover. Far less known, though, is how the tale of Sisyphus starts. It has, in fact, a number of different beginnings. Camus alludes to a few of the versions, but does not dwell on them.

Sisyphus, the son of Aeolus, god of the winds, was a trickster. Time and again, he outwitted his fellow men as well as the gods. Perhaps his greatest ruse was against Hades who, ordered by Zeus and armed with handcuffs, had come to drag Sisyphus to the underworld. Instead, Sisyphus shackled Hades when he asked the god to show him how the handcuffs worked. The absurdity of holding a god prisoner was compounded by the even greater absurdity of the consequences: while Hades was hors de combat, no one could die. This thoroughly unsatisfying predicament was resolved only when Ares, the god of war, freed Hades, caught Sisyphus, and hustled him to his fate.

Yet Sisyphus resisted even then. As Ares prepared to haul him away, Sisyphus whispered to his wife, Merope, not to bury his body. Delivered to Persephone, the wily man told the queen of the underworld that his presence there was most improper: though he was dead, his body remained unburied. Strictly speaking, Sisyphus concluded, he was on the wrong side of the River Styx. As the usually grim Persephone tried to make sense of the story, Sisyphus added that were she to give him a three-day reprieve in the world above, he would see to the irregularities and thereupon return to Hades. After the befuddled queen of the underworld agreed, Sisyphus went back to the world of sun and light; all too predictably, he then reneged on his promise. Olympus's bailiff, Hermes, tracked down, apprehended the miscreant, and bundled him off—a second time—to Hades where, as punishment for his ruses, Sisyphus was wedded to the boulder he would push up a mountainside again and again through all of eternity.[45]

What better qualifications for an absurd hero? "His scorn of the gods, his hatred of death, and his passion for life won him that unspeakable penalty in which the whole being is exerted toward accomplishing nothing."[46] Yet Camus makes no mention of Sisyphus's ploys and hoaxes, swindles and impostures—all of which loomed so large for the ancient Greeks. Instead, he writes that Homer claims Sisyphus "was the wisest and most prudent of mortals."[47]

Homer in fact does no such thing. Instead, in the *Iliad* he describes Sisyphus as the *craftiest* of men. Prudence was not his strong point, while wisdom came to him too late.

Nor does Camus note another variation on the myth: Sisyphus seduced, perhaps raped, Anticleia, the wife of Laertes and mother of the greatest trickster of them all, Odysseus. Perhaps Camus was unaware of these variants; or if he knew them, perhaps he worried that they chipped away at the heroic portrait of Sisyphus. Or, again, perhaps Camus simply did what any right-thinking ancient Greek historian, tragedian, or philosopher would have done: create a hero true to his own times, not to the past.

If the poetic fragment he left to posterity is any indication, Critias seems to have made such use of the Sisyphus myth. The ancient Greek politician, philosopher—and, not coincidentally, uncle of Plato—claimed that mortals created the gods in order to impose, through fear of divine punishment, the rule of law on society. A character in his play *Sisyphus* declares that a wise man "invented for the mortals fear of gods, so that there would be something to fear for the wicked even if they hide their actions, their words or thoughts."[48] Whether the wise man is, in fact, Sisyphus; whether he speaks these words before being punished by the gods whose existence he had denied; or whether he utters them in a cosmos empty of gods, is unclear.

Do such details—does a fuller background to Sisyphus's character—change our perception of his punishment? After all, from our perspective, rape and lawless behavior merit greater punishment than mere trickery. But from our perspective—or, for that matter, the ancient Greeks'— the gods were hardly paragons of morality or, more important, justice. What does it matter, in the end, if Sisyphus

does what he does in either a world overseen by many
gods or a world overseen by no gods at all? In either case,
a transcendental foundation is absent and there is no
absolute standard by which we can mete out punishment
to those we consider outlaws.

It is precisely a world indifferent to the acts of men that
is considered by a descendant of Sisyphus, the Homeric
hero Glaucus. A Trojan warrior, Glaucus meets his coun-
terpart Diomedes on the field of battle under the walls of
Troy. As the two men prepare to collide, Diomedes asks
Glaucus about his origins. In one of the poem's most
memorable passages, the Trojan replies:

> Why ask my birth, Diomedes? Very like leaves
> Upon this earth are the generations of men—
> Old leaves, cast on the ground by wind, young leaves
> The greening forest bears when spring comes in
> So mortals pass; one generation flowers
> Even as another dies away.[49]

When the two warriors discover they are related to one
another, they clasp arms, declare themselves friends, and
seek other foes. They have, in effect, found one of the two
sure things in a world empty of transcendence: friendship.
And they separate in pursuit of the other sure thing: glory.
Must we imagine, to anticipate the final line of the essay,
both of these men happy?

Shortly after Christmas 1940, one of the coldest France
had ever known, *Paris-Soir* gave Camus his walking papers:

economic hard times had arrived even for newspapers devoted to pap and propaganda. In a sense, the news accomplished what Camus had not himself succeeded to do:
leave a paper whose raison d'être sickened him. It also
freed him to leave a landscape that disgusted him, as well:
without a paycheck, he lost the last reason he had to stay
in metropolitan France. In early January, he and Francine
took a train to Marseilles and finally sailed home to Algeria. There was no immediate prospect of a job in Algiers,
so the couple moved to Oran, Algeria's second city, occu-
pying an apartment owned by Faure's family.

Oran was a fitting stage for this dismal period in Camus' life. The city had none of the qualities that flour-
ished in Algiers: the seamless meeting of the sea and city,
the vivacity of street life, the pulse of intellectual and artistic activity. Instead, Oran was a city determined to ignore the sea. There is nowhere, Camus despaired, "that
the people of Oran have not disfigured by some hideous
piece of building that ought by rights to destroy any
landscape."[50] As for the city itself, the streets "are doomed
to dust, pebbles, and heat. If it rains, there is a deluge and
a sea of mud." These streets fold in upon themselves,
forming a maze at whose center the pedestrian finds not
the Minotaur, but a beast far worse: boredom.[51]

Boredom was even more terrible if you did not have a
job. As Camus told one friend, returning to Oran "in
these particular conditions hardly marks a step forward."[52] Apart from a few editing jobs, Camus spent several shiftless weeks in the city. Finally, he did land a

job—one created by Vichy's anti-Semitic legislation. When a restrictive quota was placed on the number of Jewish children allowed to attend public school in France, there suddenly formed a great pool of students in desperate need of schooling. With its large Jewish community, Oran in particular needed instructors; by March, Camus was teaching at two private schools alongside Jewish friends who had been expelled from the public schools.

Camus became a jack-of-all-trades with classes ranging from French to geography to philosophy, yet none of the subjects could explain the absurdity of the situation. At the same time, Camus was equally aware of the need to respond to or overcome this condition. With his wife, he organized money collections and provided shelter for Jewish friends who had lost positions due to the racial quotas. There were guarded conversations about resistance; questions of how, when, and where were discussed, but little of substance followed. And yet the atmosphere of Oran remained thick and oppressive. Though Camus welcomed the steady income and did what he could for friends, he loathed his situation. "The days are long and weigh on me," he confided to one friend.[53] To another friend, he wrote: "I am suffocating." For a man stricken with tuberculosis, such a metaphor could not have come easily.

It was in the midst of this unsettled and unsatisfying period that Camus finished the manuscript of *The Myth of Sisyphus*. With *The Stranger* and *Caligula* already written, the "three absurds" were now done. Here, at least, was relief: after announcing in his notebook the completion of the three works, Camus sighed: "Beginnings of liberty."[54] As Camus' reworking of the myth reveals, liberty can be found in the oddest of places—even Oran or Hades.

"The gods had condemned Sisyphus to ceaselessly rolling a rock to the top of a mountain, whence the stone would fall back of its own weight. They had thought with some reason that there is no more dreadful punishment than futile and hopeless labor."[55] While his initial portrait of Sisyphus is spare, Camus subsequently fleshes out the myth. He describes Sisyphus as "straining" to raise the rock, and notes the immensity of the challenge, but all in all the vast physical effort entailed seems an afterthought for Camus. It is as if the torment inflicted by the gods has little if anything to do with a body taxed beyond measure, and everything to do with a mind challenged by the endlessly repetitive nature of the task. Condemned to repeat time and again, through all of eternity with neither a pause nor goal the same task under the gaze of a blind universe, the circumference and weight of Sisyphus's boulder is unimportant. The torment, instead, lies in the endless repetition of a meaningless chore.[56]

It would be pointless, then, to change or refine Sisyphus's task: whether it be pushing a lawnmower, threading a needle, dunking a basketball, taking out the trash, removing a comma then replacing it, the torture resides in repeating endlessly a single gesture that comes to nothing. The weight of the labor is not the consequence of gravity, but instead found in the gravity of its inconsequential nature. Sisypyhus is bound to the boulder, of course, but, more important, he is bound to the absurdity of his relationship with the boulder.

But what, Richard Taylor asks, if we were to change not the task but Sisyphus's perspective? What if the gods had perversely decided to lighten Sisyphus's punishment by giving him a drug that made him love what he was doing? That all he wanted to do with his unending life was to push a boulder up the mountainside again and again? The prisoner would thus be liberated, Taylor concludes: "If Sisyphus had a keen and unappeasable desire to be doing just what he found himself doing, then, although his life would in no way be changed, it would nevertheless have a meaning for him."[57] In response to the final line of the essay, it would thus be easy to "imagine Sisyphus happy."

Can we, though, imagine *Camus* happy with such a scenario?

Near the end of January 1942, Camus began to cough while at home with Francine. As his spasms grew more violent and blood streaked the phlegm, Francine ran out to find their doctor. The following morning the coughing had quieted, but Camus knew it was a reprieve, not a resolution. To his sister-in-law Christiane Faure he confessed: "I thought it was all over for me this time."[58] The doctor's diagnosis confirmed Camus' fear: until then only his left lung had been diseased. Now, however, the right lung was equally affected. It appeared more than ever to Camus that life was to be lived without appeal.

As Camus' tuberculosis seeped into his healthy lung, so too did Vichy's racist policies leech into everyday life in Oran. In mid-1941 the regime imposed a *numerus clausus*, or quota, on the professions: Jews were allowed to constitute just 2 percent of the total number of dentists, doctors, and lawyers in France. Camus' own doctor, Henri Cohen, was forced to give up his practice and now depended upon the kindness of colleagues who lent him their offices.

Fittingly, it was Cohen who urged Camus to undertake a different kind of exile. Worried that another damp summer in Oran would weaken Camus' lungs even further, the doctor advised his patient to spend time at a sanatorium in mainland France. Unable to afford a sanatorium, Camus settled for the solution offered by his in-laws: a farmhouse they owned near Chambon-sur-Lignon, an isolated village in the Cévennes Mountains in south-central France. In August, Albert and Francine Camus boarded a steamer at Algiers.

Once the Camus arrived in Marseilles, they boarded a series of trains, first to Lyons, then the smaller city of Saint-Etienne, and finally to Chambon-sur-Lignon. Yet even then, Camus, exhausted and short of breath, had still not reached his destination. At the rustic train station in Chambon, he and Francine hired a horse-drawn cart to take them to Le Panelier, a clump of stone farmhouses corralled by a large wall, which was the property of her family and lay a few kilometers outside the village.

Late summer in the Cévennes proved tonic for the visitor. The valleys, veined by streams and paths, were green and soothing. Though he told a friend in Algiers that it would "take much time and many walks" before feeling at home in his new surroundings, Camus was less reticent in his notebook: "The sound of babbling springs [runs] throughout my days. They flow around me, through sunny fields, then closer to me and soon I shall have this sound in me, that spring in my heart and that sound of a fountain mingled with my every thought. It's forgetfulness."[59] At times, the forces of nature themselves seemed mobilized to help in the task of "forgetfulness"—the effort to put behind his recent bout of illness. Camus compared the thick waves of fir trees to a "barbarian army of daylight" that would "drive out the fragile army of nocturnal thoughts."[60]

In early October, Francine returned to Oran; Camus planned to follow once Francine had found teaching jobs in Algiers for both of them. The weather began to turn wet and cold, most of the other boarders at the farmhouse, with whom Camus rarely spoke in any case, parted and Camus' train rides to Saint-Etienne for his pneumothorax injections remained his sole tie to the outside world—they provided, quite literally, a window onto France. Sitting against the railcar's glass pane, he studied the faces of the villagers waiting for other trains; at those stations where his train stopped, he watched his fellow travelers as they shuffled down the corridor. At the station in Saint-Etienne he observed travelers silently eat "vile fare then go out into the dark town [and] rub elbows without mingling. . . . Desolating and silent life that all France endures while waiting."[61] How could one understand France years from now, he wondered, without dwelling on these scenes? He reflected on the faces he saw "grouped in front of tiny stations . . . silhouettes I shall never forget: old peasant couples—she with a weathered face and he with a smooth face lighted by two bright eyes and a white moustache, silhouettes that two winters of privation have twisted, dressed in shiny, darned clothing. Elegance has left these people, now inhabited by poverty. On trains their suitcases are worn-out, tied with strings, patched with cardboard. All the French look like immigrants."[62]

On November 11, 1942, the wait suddenly seemed both shorter and grimmer. The Germans replied to the Allied landings in North Africa by crossing the Demarcation Line, which divided the Free and Occupied Zones established in 1940, and laying claim to the rest of France. That same day, Camus jotted in his notebook "Caught like rats!" A wall had suddenly risen up between Camus and Algeria: he could no longer return to his family, friends, and familiar landscapes. It was the situation of the absurd man: one who has only "his lucidity and his definite knowledge of the walls that surround him."[63]

The same month that Camus found himself trapped in France, he learned that sales of *The Stranger,* published earlier that year by Gallimard, justified a second run of 4,400 copies.[64] In a country where paper was increasingly precious, the publishing house's decision should have been especially welcome. Yet Camus, glad for the book's relative commercial success, was disappointed by the critical response. In a letter to his high school friend Claude de Fréminville, he dismissed both the good and mediocre reviews since they were all "based on misunderstandings" of the book. It is best, he concluded, to "shut my ears and keep working."[65]

Yet one review of the book, published in the respected *Cahiers du Sud* in early 1943, pierced Camus' mixture of frustration and indifference. In a twenty-page review—far more space than he had given to earlier reviews of writers like William Faulkner or Jean Giraudoux—the up-and-coming Jean-Paul Sartre commented on the book with striking lucidity.[66] In his review, titled "An Explication of *The Stranger*," Sartre filters Camus' novel through the insights of the philosophical essay.

Of course, Sartre does this from the position of a Parisian intellectual examining a curious artifact from a distant region. But this does not lessen his insights. Besides, *The Stranger is* a deeply curious object, one far-flung from the cafés of the Left Bank. The story of Meursault, a man whose days are a scarcely differentiated succession of sounds, sights, and sensations, a succession of discrete events he recounts in a flat voice and with scant explanation, even as he kills an Arab on an Algiers beach, and in turn is prepared to be killed by the state for his crime—two actions equally senseless—is baffling. How are we to understand this story?

It depends on what we mean by understanding, Sartre replies. We are not meant to glean meaning from this account; let us understand there is nothing to understand. Herein lies the scandal of the book, as well as the sense of its title: "The stranger he wants to portray is precisely one of those terrible 'idiots' who shock society by not accepting the rules of its game. He lives among outsiders, but to them, too, he is a stranger. . . . And we ourselves, who, on opening the book are not yet familiar with the feeling of the absurd, vainly try to judge him according to our usual standards. For us, too, he is a stranger."[67]

Perhaps the most famous image Camus uses in *The Myth of Sisyphus* to convey the senseless depths welling just below the fragile crust of our beliefs and conventions is that of a man, behind a glass partition, speaking on a phone. "You cannot hear him, but you see his incomprehensible dumb show: you wonder why he is alive."[68] In a way, Camus has stacked the ontological deck: this dumb show would crumble were we to overhear the conversation or even one side of it. Meaning would reinstall itself in a world that, for a moment, seemed deprived of it. For this reason, the philosopher Colin Wilson dismissed Camus' image as misleading: the man on the phone "has been stripped of certain essential 'clues' that would enable you to complete the picture."[69]

In his review, Sartre found this particular image flawed for the same reason: "The gesturing of the man on the telephone—whom you cannot hear—is only relatively absurd, because it is part of an incomplete circuit. But if you open the booth door and then put your ear to the receiver, the circuit is complete and the human activity makes sense again."[70] Unlike Wilson, though, Sartre recognizes that Camus is not presenting an argument, but a method— "We are dealing with a matter not of honesty, but of

art"—so as to render the world simultaneously transpar-
ent yet opaque. This particular aesthetic, in turn, reveals
a truth about the human condition that formal arguments
simply cannot: we live in a world that refuses to signify,
and thus risks transforming our acts and words into
spasms of arbitrary and senseless gestures.

These activities are no less senseless, Sartre suggests,
than the frantic rounds Voltaire puts his characters
through in his equally short and telegraphic stories. Perhaps. After all, the glass partition is, by other means, arriv-
ing at the view from nowhere. The protagonist of Voltaire's
Micromégas, a visitor from a distant planet who, since he
is 20,000 feet tall and cannot hear or see human beings,
concludes the earth is lifeless. Even if he could see us,
would our movements be at all meaningful? But the
absurdity that bathes the worlds of Candide or Micromégas is satiric: our laughter topples the rickety structure
of reactionary political and religious values that bedev-
iled Voltaire's age of enlightenment. With *The Stranger,*
however, there is no evidence that enlightenment will lead
to understanding—at least a form of understanding that
Voltaire would recognize.

Few things better concentrate the mind, of course, than
the prospect of being hanged the next day. In Meursault's
case, though, it is a question, first of all, of forming a mind.
We observe Meursault's growing self-awareness once he is
imprisoned and tried for the murder of the Arab. He grows
more reflective, but the reflection is provided by a society
that shuns him: he is an outsider who has forfeited his
right to live among men and women. The prosecuting

magistrate, who had peered into Meursault's soul, announces to a stunned jury that he had "found nothing
human."[71] Indeed, it was as if a glass partition had been
thrown between the magistrate and Meursault.

In the seclusion of his prison cell, Meursault comes to
himself. Falling asleep on his cot after a violent altercation with a visiting priest, Meursault wakens with his
face turned to a window giving onto the night sky. "For
the first time, in that night alive with signs and stars, I
opened myself to the tender indifference of the world."[72]
This scene restages the last days of Julien Sorel, the hero of
Stendhal's *The Red and Black*. References to the nineteenth-
century novelist abound in Camus' journal, many expressing wonder at Stendhal's spare style and unsparing
insights into human nature. But Camus was equally impressed by Sorel's struggle against the bog of hypocrisy
and appearance that we call society. Like Meursault confined to his cell on the eve of his execution, Julien realizes
that he knew true happiness only as an artless youth; that
he, too, once having tossed an insistent priest out of his
cell, gives himself over to his final reflections; that he, too,
in his doomed effort to find unity and meaning, instead
confronts absurdity: "A mayfly is born at nine o'clock on
the morning of a long summer day, to die at five that very
afternoon—how should it understand the word *night*?"[73]

Admittedly, we run the risk of ahistoricism by associating absurdity with Restoration France. Like any philosophical concept, the absurd was born in a specific time and place. As Terry Eagleton recently observed, while all men and women ponder the meaning of life, "some, for good historical reasons, are drawn to ponder it more urgently than others."[74] This, we have seen, was the case with France—and Camus—in 1940.

As early as 1946, however, scarcely four years after the publication of *The Stranger* and *The Myth of Sisyphus,* the philosopher A. J. Ayer, then serving in the British embassy in newly liberated Paris, began to insist on the term's limitations. In an essay on Camus, the English apostle of logical positivism dismissed the concept, in the strictest sense of the word, as nonsense. Anglo-American philosophers, Ayer observed, did not recognize the way in which Camus employed terms like "logic" and "reason." The absurd, he wrote, fell into "what modern Cambridge philosophers would call a 'pointless lament.'"[75] Nevertheless, Ayer acknowledged there was a point, unwelcome and awkward though it might be, just below the surface of Camus' prose. An undeniable "emotional significance" pulsed through the essay, Ayer confessed: "I myself happen to have considerable sympathy for the standards of value that Camus there associates with his doctrine of absurdity."[76] Moreover, he believed there was metaphysical validity to the questions asked by Camus. But this, for Ayer, is faint praise: "They are metaphysical because they are incapable of being answered by reference to any possible experience."[77]

Many years later, in his autobiography, Ayer expressed his admiration for Camus' writing and personal character: the Frenchman, he recalled, was a "man of great integrity and moral courage." His integrity seems to have been so great that at a meeting between the two men, Camus agreed with Ayer's dim view of his philosophical reasoning. In Ayer's account, Camus "demurred only to my having described him as a teacher of philosophy in his youth in Algiers, when he had in fact been a professional footballer." That Camus had never played professionally suggests that Ayer failed to understand Camus' French, his sense of humor, or perhaps both.[78] Even more clearly, Ayer also failed to understand Camus' fundamental claim in *The Myth of Sisyphus*. After all, his complacent conclusion that there can be no answer to such "metaphysical" concerns simply underscores Camus' anything but complacent "lament."

In the early 1970s, the philosopher Thomas Nagel expressed a similar mixture of condescension and concession. Most people, he noted, "feel on occasion that life is absurd, and some feel it vividly and continually." Yet the reasons given for this sensation, he continued, are "patently inadequate."[79] Echoing Ayer's formalist impatience, Nagel claimed "the standard arguments for absurdity fail as arguments."[80] Yet Nagel feels the undertow of truths that syllogisms cannot reach. Though these arguments are logically impoverished, they nevertheless "attempt to express something that is difficult to state, but fundamentally correct."[81] He allows that these failed arguments persist because they reflect something true and enduring about our lives: the shock we feel when, stepping outside ourselves and adopting "the view from nowhere," we suddenly confront the dissonance between the great importance we devote to our daily activities and their ultimate inconsequentiality. The reasons we had assumed sufficient now appear no less arbitrary than a tornado that obliterates one house yet leaves untouched the neighboring house. At this point, Nagel declares, "we see ourselves from outside, and all the contingency and specificity of our aims and pursuits become clear. Yet when we take this view and recognize what we do as arbitrary, it does not disengage us from life, and there lies our absurdity."[82]

This capacity for a view from nowhere, unique to humankind and woven into the fiber of our thought, is the boon and bane of our existences. Rather than the result of a collision between our demand for reason and the world's silence, Nagel instead puts our sense of absurdity down to a "collision within ourselves."[83] Yet this state of affairs is hardly reason for the "romantic and slightly self-pitying" posture he associates with Camus. Once we truly understand the cosmic unimportance of our situation, Nagel concludes, we ought to adopt an ironic attitude.[84]

Yet another quarter century later, Terry Eagleton in turn adopts the unruffled urbanity displayed by Ayer and Nagel. "The tragic defiance of Albert Camus, when confronted with a supposedly meaningless world, is really part of the problem to which it is a response. You are only likely to feel that the world is sickeningly pointless, as opposed to plain old pointless, if you had inflated expectations of it in the first place."[85]

Irony perhaps comes more easily to those who have lived mostly in the aftermath of World War II than those who lived through it. But the difference between Ayer, Nagel, and Eagelton on the one hand, and Camus on the other, is not just a question of style. Instead, the ironic response is the disease that pretends to be the cure. As Jeffrey Gordon suggests, Nagel's breezy treatment "may be taken as a sign of a new stage of our spiritual crisis, the stage in which, weary of our mourning, we try to persuade ourselves of the insignificance of the mourned."[86] Camus' urgency when confronted with the question of meaning, far from theatrical, is the visceral acknowledgment of the problem's dimensions. Ironic detachment is tantamount to the wearing of philosophical blinders. But to a man who puts them aside, Camus writes, "there is no finer sight than that of the intelligence at grips with a reality that transcends it. . . . To impoverish that reality whose inhumanity constitutes man's majesty is tantamount to impoverishing him himself. I understand then why the doctrines that explain everything to me also debilitate me at the same time. They relieve me of the weight of my own life."[87]

Indeed, philosophers no less than theologians or ideologues are guilty of this activity. Yet while a certain class of professional philosophers offers answers in guise of doctrines, another kind of philosopher, akin to a moralist, offers only questions. Robert Solomon observed that the arguments in *The Myth of Sisyphus* are flops. But should we insist that these arguments be construed in strictly philosophical terms? From this perspective, Camus' claims are no more rigorous or logical than Plato's. But can we thus dismiss Plato, or Camus for that matter? If we do so, is it not the reader, rather than these thinkers who betrays philosophy's raison d'être? Solomon suggested that this refusal to argue in such narrowly logical terms is what makes for the greatness of certain philosophers: "They may be trying to do something else: to make us think, to give us a vision, to inspire us to change our lives by way of many different devices, only one of which is argument."[88]

Another way is by images, be they of mythical or contemporary figures: Sisyphus on the one hand, a villager of Chambon on the other. The passage from one to the other, Camus discovers, is the passage from solitary revolt against the world's absurdity to collective revolt against man's inhumanity to man.

By late 1942, the villagers of nearby Chambon had fully assumed the weight of their own lives by accepting the weight of the lives of others. Under the leadership of their pastor, André Trocmé, the Chambonnais were acutely aware of the future that Vichy was preparing for the Jews. As early as 1940, when a dispirited nation had embraced Marshal Philippe Pétain, head of Vichy, Trocmé kept his distance, refusing in 1940 to sign the oath of allegiance to Pétain or to sound the church bells in 1941 to mark his birthday. In these and similar cases, Trocmé avoided confronting the authorities directly: holding fast to his beliefs, but not endangering his church.

All this changed, though, when a mounting stream of Jews—in 1941 they were ordered to wear the yellow star on their outer garments—quit the Occupied Zone and began to find their way to Chambon. In order to shelter these refugees, Trocmé realized that a more systematic, and much more dangerous, resistance was required. The philosopher Philip Hallie has emphasized that Trocmé and his fellow villagers were amateurs. There were no teachers, primers, or even resistance pamphlets for them to consult. Establishing lines of communication with other clandestine groups, finding safe houses and creating aliases for the refugees, and forging papers and identity cards all demanded an extraordinary degree of planning and care. Yet, the practical and organizational aspects to the work of saving the lives of others always remained a work in progress.

Equally significant, however, were the less practical elements of resistance. While the villagers groped toward developing an effective organization, they did not hesitate over the need to resist. Their clarity of vision resulted in part from the historical experience of the Huguenot community, but, no less important, it reflected an ethical stance that Trocmé had practiced his entire adult life. Resistance is, first and foremost, a way of seeing the world, one that makes manifest the moral imperative to acknowledge and respect the dignity of each and every fellow human being.

As a result, by the time their fellow Frenchmen and women began to grasp Vichy's brutal nature, the Chambonnais already knew what to do. This applied to something as seemingly simple as refusing to sign an oath of allegiance, or to something far greater—such as when the village youths delivered a letter to a visiting government minister, declaring they would never accept the regime's actions against Jews. And, of course, it applied to saving the lives of the more than 3,000 Jewish adults and children by placing them with families, hiding them in the region or spiriting them out of the country. As Iris Murdoch wrote, seeing the world with consistent clarity means that when the moment arrives to make a moral choice, the choice has already been made.[89]

Perhaps absurdity has not aged at all. Take Job. We think we know the biblical story—until we recall the story wedged between its opening and ending. If we read only the first and last chapters, we meet the man with whom we are all familiar: the man in the land of Uz who is rewarded for his infinite store of patience and faith in God. If we read the forty chapters in between, however—passages that scholars believe to be older than the opening and closing chapters—we meet a man up against a cosmic order that obliterates every belief he had held about it.

Recall the setting: When God praises his servant Job, his Adversary—the name Robert Alter gives Satan in his translation[90]—makes a bet: if you claw back everything you have given the man, I bet he will curse you. God accepts the Adversary's wager and all hell breaks loose in Job's earthly life. He loses his flocks, his servants, and, most important, his children. As a final kick to Job's crumpled body, the Adversary—with God's consent, of course—then "smote him with sore boils from the sole of his foot until his crown." Like the three friends who come to mourn with Job, readers want to weep as well, perhaps even rend their clothing and sprinkle dirt on their heads, then sit in silence for seven days. We need at least that much time, it seems, to try to understand the moral and philosophical dimensions of this tale. Where does this chain of catastrophes, undeserved and unexplained, leave Job? It leaves him, quite simply, sitting on a mound of ashes, scraping off his boils with a shard of pottery while searching for an answer.

Job turns first to his friends for an answer; in their various ways, they insist that, given God's nature, Job's punishment must be just. For Job, though, this response is not just slanderous—he knows he has done nothing to deserve his God's wrath—but also a failure of moral imagination. The friends cling to a certain stage setting—namely, their belief in a world ordered by divine justice—all the more desperately as Job, through his words and experience, reveals the sheer emptiness of this conviction. Halfway through the story, Job dismisses the possibility of consolation, much less understanding, from his friends. They have instead made him a "stranger" and "an alien in their sight."

Tragically, the heavens seem no less determined to estrange Job. While he pursues his litany of questions, the skies remain mute. As he cries out, "Behold, I cry out of wrong, but I am not heard: I cry aloud, but there is no judgment. He hath fenced up my way that I cannot pass, and he hath set darkness in my paths." The silence of the world, in effect, only becomes silence when human beings enter the equation. All too absurdly, Job demands meaning; no less absurdly, he must ask himself what he must do if meaning is not to be found? What is his next step if meaning fails to show up at the appointed rendez-vous? "But where shall wisdom be found?/And where is the place of understanding?"

The problem for Job, paradoxically, ultimately resides less in God's silence than in his words. Finally roused, God speaks through a whirlwind, demanding who it is that "darkeneth counsel by words without knowledge? Gird up now thy loins like a man; for I will demand of thee, and answer thou me. Where wast thou when I laid the foundations of the earth? Declare, if thou hast under-standing." The storm-tossed voice launches dozens of sim-ilar questions, all of them equally irrelevant to Job's quest for meaning. By the end of this battering, Job confesses that he had no right to demand to know the reasons why he suffered. The sheer incommensurability between God's perspective and Job's, it seems, is reason enough.

At the end of the day, Job discovers he lives in a stripped and bare world whose strangeness and opacity beggar any effort at comprehension. In response to his demand for answers, he first gets silence, followed by words that deny the possibility of meaningfulness. Job, of course, submits. Herein lies the absurdity. Is there, in the end, a difference between the silence of Camus' cosmos and the sound and fury of God's reply? The words that spin out of the whirl-wind are irate and implacable, but one need not be Mar-tin Buber to realize that God never answers Job's insis-tence for a meaning to all that has happened. The author of Job leaves us with the same feeling as does the author of Sisyphus: there is no meaning to be had. Rather than breathing a sigh of relief with the Job who is rewarded by God for his loyalty, we instead must contend with a Job who answers God's deafening and dismal effort at self-justification with silence.

In fact, Martin Buber suggests that Job, having failed in his pursuit for justice in the world, finds it only within himself. With the story of Job, Buber continues, we "witness the first clothing of a human quest in form of speech."[91] The silent Job, not the groveling Job, is Camus' Job—and perhaps the original author's Job, as well. As Jack Miles points out, after this book, God never again speaks in the Bible. God's last words, he notes, "are those he speaks to Job, the human being who dares to challenge not his physical power, but his moral authority . . . reading from the end of the Book of Job onward, we see that it is Job who has somehow silenced God."[92]

In the end, we have two different wisdom books, two different authors, but they perhaps both offer the same lesson.

But how relevant was this lesson in wartime France? In the isolation of Le Panelier, Camus seemed sheltered from the extraordinary events slowly unfolding in Chambon. There is no direct trace in his notebooks or correspondence that reveals knowledge about the rescue activities just down the road from the farmhouse. This, perhaps, is natural: if Camus did not know about these activities, he could not recount them; if he did know, he *would not* recount them for reasons of security. While family members do not recall any mention made by Camus of events in Chambon, a number of contemporaries claim that Camus was at the very least aware of the undertaking. After all, some of the pensioners at Le Panelier were themselves Jewish refugees. This is just one reason why André Chouraqui, Camus' guide to the Hebrew Bible, insisted that his friend "had always known about the resistance Pastors Trocmé and Theis conducted in Le Chambon-sur-Lignon."[93] Yet another reason is that the names of several characters in the novel he was now drafting, *The Plague,* parallel the names of local figures. Most notably, the novel's narrator (and hero), Dr. Rieux, seems to be based on the doctor at Chambon, Dr. Riou.

In the end, however, questions along the lines of "What did he know and when did he know it?" are simply irrelevant. For whatever reason, by late 1942 Camus had begun to reconsider the limits of absurdity. In his notebooks, he wondered what the world would make of a thinker who suddenly announced: "Up to now I was going in the wrong direction. I am going to begin all over." The world, of course, would laugh at him. But this must not dissuade an honest thinker. Instead, it offers additional proof that "he is worthy of thought."[94] This new stage of reflection accepted the fact that the world is absurd—an unavoidable diagnosis of the human condition. But at the same time, Camus realized it was nothing more than a diagnosis. Hence his confession in the preface to the American edition of the *Myth* that the fundamental concerns that drove him to write the *Myth of Sisyphus* were still present.

Though he had "progressed beyond several of the positions which are set down" in the book, Camus wrote, "I have remained faithful, it seems to me, to the exigency which prompted them."[95]

The absurd, Camus wrote in 1942, "*teaches* nothing."[96] Instead of looking at ourselves, as do Sisyphus, Meursault, or even Job, we must look to others: we are, Camus recognized, condemned to live together in this silent world. When a Vichy official ordered André Trocmé to tell him the whereabouts of the refugee Jews, the pastor replied: "We do not know what a Jew is. We know only men."[97] During the same period, Camus echoes this sentiment: "The misery and greatness of this world: it offers no truths, but only objects for love. Absurdity is king, but love saves us from it."[98]

2

SILENCE

In the beginning, there was silence. At the end of an overnight train trip in a third-class compartment from the capital Algiers, the husband and wife, several months pregnant, arrived in Bône, a small city on the northeast coast of Algeria. While his wife watched, the man helped an Arab driver load their few bags onto a horse-drawn wagon waiting to take them to the farm that the husband had been hired to manage. The jarring trip on the potholed and rain-soaked roads hastened the pregnancy, for the wife began to have labor pains on the wagon. By the time the travelers reached their destination, the woman was "weeping silently" from pain. The local doctor arrived, a makeshift bed was placed in front of the fireplace, and a boy was born. As the rain tailed off, the infant and his parents fell asleep in the silence of their new home.

Or, perhaps, in the beginning was the word. Camus' account of his own birth, which begins his last and uncompleted novel *The First Man,* seems based on a family account. How could it be otherwise? No one is a witness to his or her own birth. Saint Augustine, who finished his life as bishop of Hippo (as Bône was then known), begins the *Confessions* with an account of his birth. But, as he immediately observes, he cannot himself testify to it. Instead, he must depend on the accounts of others: "I have heard from the parents of my flesh, from where and in whom you fashioned me in time; for I myself do not remember."[1]

In the *Confessions,* "the other North African," as Camus gently referred to Augustine, tries to understand his origins. So, too, does Camus in his last work. Augustine questions God about the world and about himself, but receives silence in return. In like fashion, the hero of Camus' novel, Jacques Cormery, questions his own past and meets little more than silence. From the silence that surrounds his birth, Cormery moves to the silence that surrounds his father's death. Killed in 1914 at the Battle of the Marne when his youngest son was scarcely a year old, Lucien Camus left behind little. Splinters from the shell that were removed from his skull; a Croix de guerre; an official letter announcing his death; a blurred photograph of a young man with almond-shaped eyes: the shards left by his father's life.

Like so many other *pieds-noirs,* Lucien Camus had been buried in the soil of metropolitan France; in his case, a military cemetery in Saint-Brieuc, a small city in Brittany. In 1947, Camus visited the cemetery in the company of the novelist Louis Guilloux, who lived just outside the city. The older writer took Camus to the area reserved for the military, staying behind while Camus walked to a simple stone slab engraved with his father's name and dates of birth and death. When he returned to Guilloux, Camus did not say a word. In *The First Man,* though, Camus recreates this visit: as Cormery stares "vacantly" at the stone, he noticed clouds scudding above him. All around, "in the vast field of the dead, silence reigned. Nothing but a muffled murmur from the town came over the high walls." It is only when Cormery hears "the clink of a bucket against the marble of a tombstone" that his reverie is broken. He then sees, as if for the first time, the dates under his father's name: "1885-1914." His silence deepens with the realization that the "man buried under that slab, who had been his father, was younger than he."

This shock loosens a surge of memories, most of which are steeped in silence. His own youth had always "strained toward that goal which he knew nothing about"; suddenly, everything seem tied to this man about whom he knew only that he resembled him. But what could he do? "In a family where they spoke little, where no one read or wrote, with an unhappy and listless mother, who would have informed him about this young and pitiable father?"[2]

In his idiosyncratic but often compelling work *The World of Silence,* Max Picard insists that silence is not simply negative—the mere absence of speech or what we do *not* hear when others stop talking, machines stop whirring, radios and screens stop making noise. On the contrary, it exists independently of language and noise; it is a "a complete world in itself. Silence has greatness simply because it is. It is, and that is its greatness, its pure greatness."[3]

Picard's observation that silence, though neither visible nor defined, nevertheless has a palpable and definite presence in the world, infuses Camus' recollections of his childhood. Camus' grandmother, Catherine Marie Cardona Sintes, had taken in his mother, him, and his older brother when Lucien went to war. With his death, their temporary quarters, located in the working-class neighborhood of Belcourt, became permanent. A widowed, rough matriarch, Catherine Sintes was illiterate and laconic. At times, rather than speaking or shouting, she instead struck, slapped, or whipped Camus and his older brother Lucien.

One of the grandmother's sons, Etienne, also lived in the apartment. Like his sister Catherine, this powerfully built man could not hear and spoke only with difficulty. A cooper by trade, Etienne would take Camus to the workshop where he fashioned barrels or the countryside for a Sunday hunting expedition. About his past, all Camus could learn from Etienne was the son had a "hard head" like his father: "Did what he wanted, always." Unable to express himself through words, Etienne instead made an astonishing variety of noises to convey his meaning.[4]

Etienne would also perform elaborate pantomimes—a silent form of storytelling that was not limited to the family apartment. On Sunday afternoons, the young Camus would accompany his grandmother to the local movie house. The movies were silent, but not wordless: many frames carried dialogue or captions. Unable to read, the grandmother expected Camus to read aloud at these moments—a difficult task when speaking too loudly disturbed the other moviegoers, but speaking too softly disturbed his grandmother. Caught in this vise of conflicting demands, the child would sometimes fall silent. This once sparked his grandmother's rage; unable to understand the movie, she walked out of the theater, followed by a tearful Camus, "distressed at the thought that he had spoiled one of the poor woman's rare pleasures and that it had been paid out of their meager funds."[5]

But the deepest source of silence in Camus' life, as enduring as it was elusive, as distant as it was enveloping, was Catherine Sintès. When the young Camus returned to the apartment, his mother often was already there. And yet, she was not there. Seated on a chair by the window, she would look out silently. "Sometimes people would ask her: 'What are you thinking?' And she would answer: 'Nothing.' And it was quite true. . . . She is thinking of nothing. Outside, the light, the noises; here, silence in the night."[6] In this early essay, titled "Between Yes and No," Camus confesses that his mother's "animal silence makes him want to cry with pain." Pity floods his heart, but is this the same as love? Could he love someone who had never kissed or hugged him? Standing at the doorway, Camus gazes at his mother and glimpses a deep suffering, yet his mother, deaf and preoccupied with unfathomable thoughts, is unaware of her son's presence. "The silence marks a pause, an immensely long moment. Vaguely aware of this, the child thinks the surge of feeling in him is love for his mother. And it must be, because after all she is his mother."[7]

It was said that Camus' mother spoke easily as a young woman, just as it was thought that the shock at her husband's death during the Battle of the Marne left her with a halting tongue. What is certain, though, is that Catherine, with her sons Albert and Lucien in tow, moved into her mother's apartment in Belcourt. She spent the rest of her life there as a cleaning woman. Her words were rare; most often she spoke only when addressed by others, and even then in brief phrases. But her presence, much like a sun that cannot be seen, exercised a tremendous pull on her son—a sun that radiated an effulgent silence that he carried his entire life.

Even more than the sea, the figure of the silent mother occupies the center of Camus' writings: it is the sun, or perhaps the dark matter, toward which everything else is pulled. It is the death of Meursault's mother that begins the unmaking of his life; it is the mostly wordless presence of Rieux's mother that prevents the unmaking of a world swept by plague; it is under the silent gaze of his mother that Cormery begins the search for his past. As he began to sketch *The First Man* in the last years of his life, Camus described the novel as a "journey in order to discover his secret: he is not the first. Every man is the first man, nobody is. This is why he throws himself at his mother's feet."

Shortly before his death, Camus described his literary goal: to write a book whose center would be "the admi-

rable silence of a mother and one man's effort to rediscover a justice or a love to match this silence."[8] I am not
sure what Camus meant by this claim. It suggests that
the depths of maternal silence can, in fact, never be fully
plumbed by a son. In his notes to *The Last Man,* Camus
struggles with the fact that all of his writing, all of his
work, is for a woman who could not read and would talk
little. What he "wanted most in the world, which was for
his mother to read everything that was his life and his
being, that was impossible. His love, his only love, would
forever be speechless."[9]

Rather than the consequence of human expectations, the
absence we encounter when our ears strain, but fail to
hear something, it is instead a positive force, one far older
than humankind, perhaps older than the world itself. In
Camus' fiction and essays, the world frames this primordial silence; landscapes are soundless stages; deserts,
mountains, plateaus, and coasts serve to underscore the
silence that existed prior to man's arrival.

In early 1937, the Théâtre du travail, an amateur theater group in Algiers, staged a production of Aeschylus's
Prometheus Bound. Inspired by the Communist ideal of
bringing art to the working class, mostly young and
middle-class students and artists formed the group in
1935. Camus was the great exception; child of the working class neighborhood of Belcourt, the young student
was the defining force behind the troupe. Deeply engaged
in the city's political life—during this period he briefly

belonged to the Algerian Communist Party—Camus saw
the stage as a means to act in the world as well as before
an audience. After staging André Malraux's *Le Temps du
mépris* in 1936, Camus decided to turn to Aeschylus. As
with the Malraux piece, unemployed workers were invited to attend for free and share in the gate proceeds.

One wonders not only what they made of the tragedy's
tale—Prometheus aids man by giving him fire to achieve
his freedom, then is punished by his fellow gods—but
also of the startling stage design and costumes. All the
actors wore masks except for Prometheus, who was dressed
entirely in black. Camus assumed the task of adapting the
extant but "very heavy" French translations for the production.[10] Not surprisingly, his Prometheus seems less
preoccupied by the fate of humankind—humans are free
and freely inventing, after all, thanks to the gift of fire—
than his own eternal torment. He demands that nature
witness his punishment, but does not know how to speak
of it: "How can I find the words to describe this force de-
stroying me, but how can I remain silent about it?"[11]
Needless to say, Nature does not reply—at least in words.
Instead, the play ends with Prometheus laid bare to the
"biting winds."

Like a solar eclipse, two orbs of silence overlap: the
blinding and incommunicable reality of Prometheus's
pain and the shadow cast by an indifferent and mute
world. Time and again, Prometheus is caught between the
urge to speak and the realization that to do so is pointless: "But what shall I say? I know in advance exactly everything that will happen." Then, again: "It is painful for me

to say these things, but it is painful also to be silent ..."
These silences surge, in part, from Prometheus's failure to
find words adequate to the tasks at hand; they spell the
breakdown of language. But they also foretell a different
and greater silence that waits upon Prometheus, one that
beggars the imagination of mortals, a world where he will
not find "voice or shape of man."

Later that same year, Camus encountered this greater
silence carried on the biting wind at the Roman ruins of
Djémila. In a plane piloted by Marie Viton, a friend and
fellow member of the Théâtre du Travail, Camus flew to
this ancient place, buried in the Atlas Mountains 200
miles east of Algiers. As a sharp wind sliced relentlessly
across his face and arms, Camus was struck by a "great
and seamless silence resembling a scale's balance."[12] But
the silence was made, not unmade, by the sounds of birds
and sheep—"so many noises which made for the silence
and desolation of this place."

But such desolation is welcomed, not rejected: this site
of silence and savage wind reveals essential truths about
the human condition. At Djémila "the spirit dies in order
to give birth to a truth which is its very negation." Something takes shape within this dizzying vortex of wind
and sun, something that whips across the ruins and "gives
to man the measure of his identity with the solitude and
silence of this dead city." Never had he so deeply felt, he
later wrote, "both detachment from myself and my presence in the world."[13]

The silence Camus found at Djémila dissolved thoughts
and concerns about the future; the ruins framed not just

light and space, but also the wind-swept calm. "Among the columns of lengthening shadows, worries fell from the sky like wounded birds and were replaced by an arid lucidity." Given over entirely to himself, Camus felt defenseless against these "deep forces rising within me that said 'no.'" No, in a word, to plans for the future, to talk about tomorrow, to things not yet done. Instead, Camus demands the weight of the present, of the earth, of a world shorn of its myths and faith in anything other than what we can see and touch and feel. "Men worthy of the name will, at the end of their lives, reject the ideas they once accepted and recover the innocence and truth that shone in the eyes of ancient men facing their destiny."[14] This destiny is reflected in the fates of Prometheus and Sisyphus: to accept what they have done, embrace what they have been given, and survey silently a silent universe.

Two years later Camus collided with a very different kind of silence, one that hid rather than revealed fundamental truths about the human condition. There are moments, notes Stuart Sim, that silence matters a great deal "because noise is a signifier of ideological power."[15]

In 1938, Camus joined the staff of a newly launched newspaper, *L'Alger républicain*. Though he had never worked as a journalist, Camus shared the militant paper's goal of unmasking the economic inequities and social iniquities suffered by urban and rural workers, Arab and Berber no less than *pied-noir*. In the early summer of 1938, the editor of the paper, Pascal Pia, sent Camus to Kabylia, a mountainous region east of Algiers.

Berbers farmed the rocky soil, living in villages perched on mountaintops, surviving on the fig and olive orchards that clung to the slopes. During France's "pacification" of this region, *pied-noir* settlers seized great swathes of the arable valleys. Pushed up and out, the Berbers either retreated to their mountain villages or emigrated to the mother country. As a prod to emigration, the French state imposed a collection of cruel laws on the local population—the *Code de l'indigénat*. Under these laws, it was illegal to insult French officials, defame the government, or travel without an official permit. The French Republic, in addition, dusted off the feudal practice of corvée, forcing the Berbers to work land that was once theirs without pay or compensation.

Camus knew about these practices, but in the way he knew about the Battle of the Marne. It was unjust, but it was also distant—indeed, distant enough to allow him to idealize the Algerian landscape in his early essays without the encumbrance of desperate and uprooted people. For the young Camus who had not yet visited Kabylia, nature in its benign severity forced us to confront life in its stark simplicity: "Between this sky and the faces turned toward it there is nothing on which to hang a mythology, a literature, an ethic, or a religion—only stones, flesh, stars, and those truths the hand can touch."[16]

But such idealizations were no longer possible once Camus reached Kabylia in early June. He encountered a new and deepened understanding of this world of stone and silence from a hill he had climbed with a Berber friend. Distracted from the starry depths of night sky, Camus notices fires begin to blaze in Tizi Ouzou, the village lying at the foot of the hill. Looking at his companion, Camus suddenly recalled the purpose of these fires: they are not the final touches to a sublime moment, but the sole source of energy for impoverished and starving villagers. Camus remains wordless and his companion must break the silence: "Shall we go down?"[17]

What he found upon descending eclipsed his earlier soundings of rural Algeria. Once again, Camus encountered the staggering distance between word and facts. His earlier perception of silence as a condition crucial to self-understanding is overtaken by the recollection that silence also serves political and ideological ends. The official distribution of grain, he had known, did not meet the needs of the population. "But what I did not know is that these shortages were killing people."[18] He also knew that thistle stems were a staple of the local diet, but he did not know that five children in a single district had died from eating the poisonous roots.[19] He knew, as well, that the salaries of the fortunate Berbers who had jobs was inadequate, but did not know the sums were insulting; and he knew that workers labored more than the law allowed, but not that it was nearly double the limit.[20] The reports shattered a damning silence on the plight of Berbers, leaving in tatters the standard excuse of imperial apologists: all of this was due to Berber "mentality," the bundle of local traditions and customs that threw a wall between these benighted souls and France's civilizing mission. Nonsense, replied Camus. It was a question of water, food, roads and schools—all of which Kabylia sorely lacked and French authorities did not supply.

In a dozen articles sent from Kabylia, Camus tried to pierce the silence in which this tragedy was slowly unfolding. The situation, he exclaimed, "cries for our attention, it despairs of getting it."[21] Marveling at the abyss between the ideals of the Republic and reality of Kabylia, Camus refused to surrender his ideals. The practice of separate and unequal education had to end and schools to be integrated. Silence, he understood, resulted in part from the inability of the Berbers to express their discontent in the language of the colonizer. The people of Kabylia, Camus wrote, will have "more schools the day we do away with the artificial barriers separating the European and indigenous systems of education." Only then, by sitting at the same desks will "two peoples made to live together come to know one another."[22]

In the end, Camus assumed the duty of speaking for *les muets,* the voiceless ones, silenced by administrative fiat and codified violence. France had to practice, not simply preach republicanism—an ideology that rendered France's imperial heritage so problematic, but also so promising. If France's "colonial conquests were ever to find their justification, it is to the degree that it allows the conquered peoples to keep their identities. If we have but one duty in this country, it is to permit a people so proud and humane to remain true to itself and its destiny."[23]

It was naive, from our perspective, for Camus to assume that the Berber destiny would dovetail with France's, just as it was perhaps naive to believe that this destiny would be expressed in French. Equally naive was Camus' belief that to see was to believe—and that belief would lead to practical policy. Camus wrote that if French politicians, regardless of political affiliation, took the same itinerary he had in Kabylia, the solution would be at hand. But such naiveté must not obscure Camus' heartfelt insistence upon the universal bonds of fraternity embodied by the Republic. More important, his naiveté, if that is the word, flowed from a simple, but not simplistic ethical orientation: seeing rightly is a prerequisite to acting rightly. Camus recounted a visit he makes to a *gourbi*, or hut, in the village of Adni. In a "dim and smokey room, I was welcomed by two women, one quite aged, the other pregnant. Three children stare uncomprehendingly at me.... I don't see a single piece of furniture. Only after my eyes grow accustomed to the darkness do I see signs of human life: three great basins of white clay, and two earthen bowls." When Camus asks the pregnant woman, who is "cradling her enormous stomach," where she slept, she "pointed to the earthen floor under my feet, next to a drain serving as toilet."[24]

Camus was no less attached to the silence of the *pied-noir* settlers of these same regions. In *The First Man*, Jacques Cormery vainly pursues traces of his father, an immigrant to Algeria, across the "immense and hostile land." His father made the voyage to Algeria like his fellow "conquerors" who, piled in the holds of old ships, disembarked in a land where they "melted into the anonymous history of the village and the plain."[25] These "conquerors" worked the land and were reclaimed by land, digging "deeper and deeper in some places, shakier and shakier in others, until the dusty earth covered them over and the place went back to its wild vegetation; and they had procreated, then disappeared." These generations of conquerors, Cormery reflected, "had disappeared without a trace, locked within themselves. An enormous oblivion spread over them ... dying in silence and away from everything."[26]

In the end, the settlers are as faceless and nameless, as anonymous as the Arabs in his earlier work. Does this mean that Camus is as indifferent to the one population as he is to the other? Or, instead, does it mean he believes that the powerful have exploited both peoples, who were then quietly forgotten by history?

In 1952, Paris—or, perhaps, only its Left Bank—was consumed by the fiery collapse of the friendship between Camus and Sartre. The nominal cause was a sharp, caustic, and not entirely unfair review that had appeared in *Les Temps modernes* of Camus' *The Rebel*. The monthly journal, edited by Sartre, Simone de Beauvoir, and Maurice Merleau-Ponty, had quickly shouldered its way to the top of the literary and philosophical mountain of intellectual journals in postwar France. Though he was close to the editorial board, Camus had from the start kept a certain distance from its operations. The critical distance widened into a dizzying chasm upon the publication of *The Rebel*.

In retrospect, the ideological collision between Camus and Sartre seems to have been no less determined than Prometheus's own fate. Perhaps Camus sensed what was in store when, in December 1951, he wrote in his journal: "I await with patience a catastrophe that is slow in coming."[27] *The Rebel* had just appeared and its impact was immediate and controversial. The essay's denunciation of the blind allegiance of French Communists, along with intellectuals who had either joined the party or traveled in its company, was merciless and crystallizing. Camus lashed out against the French Left's tendency to close its eyes to crimes committed in the Soviet Union in the name of historical necessity, horrified by the various intellectual arguments offered to justify the existence of slave camps and the reign of terrorism. The logic of historical events, Camus insisted, "from the moment it is totally accepted, gradually leads it . . . to mutilate man more and more and to transform itself into objective crime."[28]

Yet, for Sartre, it was the logic of Camus' analysis that transformed, if not traduced, the aims of Communism. By the time *The Rebel* was published, France's most influential thinker had concluded that circumstances demanded collective struggle rather than individual diffidence. Intellectuals did not have the luxury of standing to one side of historical necessity. Indeed, any effort to do so made one not just a bystander, but instead a veritable obstacle to the march of progress. Sartre chided Camus for this willful innocence: "You decided against history; and rather than interpret its course, you preferred to see it only as one more absurdity." This would not do: "To merit the right to influence men who are struggling, one must first participate in their struggle, and this first means accepting many things if you hope to change a few of them."[29]

More wounding for Camus than Sartre's criticism of the book was his salvo of lacerating and intimately personal insults. In the pages of *Les Temps modernes* Sartre ridiculed what he claimed were Camus' personal flaws. Because of his former friend's "mixture of somber self-conceit and vulnerability," no one had before dared to speak frankly to Camus. "The result is that you have become the victim of a bleak immoderation which masks your internal difficulties and which you call, I believe, Mediterranean measure. Sooner or later someone would have told you; let it be me."[30]

Sartre's reply staggered Camus. In the privacy of his journal he furiously reflected on the situation, convinced that the weight of ideological aspirations had forced Sartre and his followers to engage with Communism. "But there is no royal path to servitude. There is cheating, insult, denunciation of the brother."[31] Yet on the same pages, interspersed with his tormented thoughts on his own worth as a writer and thinker, are reflections that Camus made during a trip at the end of the year to the far-flung southern districts of Algeria. This truly "royal" landscape, unedited by man-made ruins as at Djémila, offered its vast silence as a balm to the fury of the jungle he knew in Paris.[32]

Driving alone from Algiers to Laghouat in mid-December, Camus discovered a desert unlike the northern one that rippled across the Roman columns at Djémila. In this oasis town, he found a "singular impression of power and invulnerability," the work of nature, not man. Even the cemetery in town, he noted, was "covered with shards of schist and the dead intermingle beneath the confusion of stones." As he pushed further south, Camus was overwhelmed by the starkly hostile landscape. Yet this particular hostility was unlike the hostility he knew in Paris; it was a grander sort, one utterly indifferent to his presence. In this "kingdom of stones" Camus reveled in the limits imposed by nature. This was no place for illusions or dreams: "when one plows in this country, it is to gather stones."

Yet this was not an invitation to romanticize this world: the silence radiating from the desert, warned Camus, also muffled the moral distress of its inhabitants. Struck by drought, tens of thousands of sheep were dying. The figures working the land were hardly picturesque; instead, an "entire populace scrapes the soil in search of roots." By the time he arrived in the village of Ghardaïa, Camus was as stunned by the human misery as he was by the relentless sun. Alone, he blurted out to his journal: "Buchenwald under the sun."[33] Though distant from Kabylia, Camus' drive into the Saharan desert revealed that silence not only reflected a kind of inhuman majesty but also collaborated in forms of human injustice. Framed by endless horizons, filled with blinding light and preternatural calm, Camus claimed this world of "silence and solitude" as a source of truth.[34] But it was a truth that had to be defended by those with voices that could be heard.

The story is simplicity itself: a group of men who work at a small producer of wooden barrels return to their workplace after a twenty-day strike that has failed. Yvars, the story's protagonist, reflects on events as he cycles to work. He has just turned forty, and a life of harsh physical labor has taken its toll: "At forty, you aren't done for, no, but you're preparing for it in advance."[35] Yvar's thoughts about the unsuccessful strike for higher wages have deepened this sense of a life winding down; he is, he realizes, ceding his place in the world. He understands that his employer, Lassalle, is in a tough bind. The demand for wooden barrels was shrinking and, in order to maintain his profit margin, Lassalle cannot afford to raise salaries. And what would happen if the entire atelier went under? "A man doesn't change trades when he's taken the trouble to learn one, and a difficult one, demanding a long apprenticeship." Giving up his trade was unthinkable, but so too was resigning himself to an inadequate paycheck and knowing his labor was undervalued. In so unforgiving a situation, "it was difficult to close your mouth."[36]

Yet, by the time he reaches the workshop, this is precisely what Yvars and his fellow workers will do. As he lifts his stiff body off the bicycle, he sees his comrades standing silently in front of the locked doors. As they wait for the foreman, Ballester, to open the door—he deliberately keeps them waiting to underscore their powerlessness—they do not exchange a word. Nor do they as they file into the workshop that suddenly seems abandoned, or when they take up their tools and begin to hammer, saw, and rivet. As they regain the rhythm of their lives prior to the strike, Lassalle appears at the threshold of the door. As Yvars recognizes, his boss—himself the son of an artisan—has always been fair and sympathetic with his workers. But something else, more diffuse, yet no less crucial has been broken along with the strike. Trying hard to appear natural, Lassalle walks slowly through

the factory and greets a few of the workers. All he receives, though, is silence. Finally, he looks at the workers,
pleading: "We don't agree, okay. But we still have to work
together. So what's the point? What good does this do?"

There is a point, though—one that is driven home a few
minutes later. Faced with the mute resistance of his workers, Lassalle walks out and returns to his house, which
doubles as his office. Through Ballester, he then sum-
mons Yvars and Marcou, the union delegate, to his office.
As they approach the door, the men hear a child crying
and Lassalle reassuring his wife that if their daughter
did not improve he would call the doctor. When Yvars
and Marcou enter the office, Lassalle assures them he
will bolster their salaries the moment business improves.
All he asks in return is for relations to continue as they
were before the strike. The workers refuse to reply, however, just as they refuse to shake his hand. Suddenly los-
ing the calm he has maintained until then, Lassalle
shouts at their backs as they leave the office: "You can all
go to Hell!"[37]

They instead return to the workshop, where the others
have already begun their meager lunches. As Yvars pulls a
sandwich out of his lunch bag, he notices Said, an Arab
who works alongside him, reclining in a pile of wood
shavings, slowly eating a few figs. Giving half of the sandwich to Said, Yvar tells him that things will get better:
"You'll invite me then." Unwittingly, Yvars has repeated
the same sentiment offered just moments earlier by
Lassalle—with the difference that, this time, the extended
hand is accepted.

Soon after they return to work, Lassalle starts to ring the work bell in a way that strikes Yvars as odd and insistent. Ballester responds, only to rush back through moments later, hurrying into town for a doctor. The owner's daughter, the workers discover, has suddenly collapsed to the floor. As the pealing of an ambulance siren grows and fades outside the workshop, the men continue to work in silence. Yvars wants to speak, but neither he nor the others have any words inside them to utter. Nor do they when Lassalle appears at the end of the workday, his hair disheveled and his gaze awkward. After a long and embarrassed silence, Lassalle mutters "Goodnight" and closes the door behind him without getting a reply. "They should have called to him," thinks Yvars, but by then it is already too late.

"Les Muets," the French title of the story, has been variously translated as "The Silent Ones" and "The Voiceless," but is best understood as the "The Mute Ones." Along with his coworkers, Yvars finds himself thrown into a state of muteness. He has no more planned to be silent in front of Lassalle—who, he admits, has always treated him fairly—than he has planned to reach the age of forty and, as he bicycles wearily to work, has found himself looking away from the sea he had loved as a youth. Rather than Yvars falling silent, silence falls over Yvars and the others. Try as he might, he could find neither the words nor, if he had found them, the will to utter them. In Lassalle's office, upon hearing the offer made by their employer, Yvars, "his teeth clenched, wanted to speak but could not."[38] So, too, the realization that he should have said something after Lassalle, devastated by his daughter's illness, briefly appeared in the workshop.

The silence at the workshop echoes a more celebrated silence heard during the Occupation, one that influenced Camus.[39] In 1941, the clandestine publishing house Editions du Minuit distributed the novella, *Le Silence de la mer*. Written by Vercors, the pen name of Jean Bruller, one of the publishing house's founders, the story recounts the relationship between a German officer, Werner von Ebrennac, and a Frenchman and his niece at whose farmhouse he is billeted. Cultivated, cultured and fluent in French, the officer enters the farmhouse's living room at the end of each day and reflects aloud to the couple. But his conversations are one-sided for neither the uncle nor his niece respond to him. The uncle smokes a pipe and gazes at the ceiling while his niece, much like Penelope, never lifts her eyes as she knits. Indeed, like Yvars and his fellow artisans, the uncle and niece have never discussed, much less planned this response. Instead, "by a silent agreement" they continued to live their lives as if the officer did not exist.[40]

In occupied France and the Algiers workshop, a silence born in humiliation slowly becomes a silence braced by the nearly instinctive insistence on dignity. Silence at such moments is not willed, but is instead visceral. It reminds us that silence preceded language and presupposes an older world in which language did not yet filter our response to it. As Picard noted, silence can exist without speech, but speech cannot exist without silence.[41] Camus' friend, the novelist Louis Guilloux, phrased this differently: "Ultimately, we do not write in order to say things, but in order not to say them."[42] Today we tend to regard silence as the interruption of noise, but once we recover from the effects of sound, we realize that silence's primordial function is to provide a kind of basso continuo to the drama of our lives.

But while Yvars, like Vercors' characters, remain mute in the face of their insistent interlocutors, their silence cannot be maintained. The niece and uncle ultimately respond to von Ebrennac after he learns that he alone among his fellow officers dreams of a marriage between the German and French cultures. Unable to bear the shock of discovering what the Nazis have in store for France, he requests a transfer to the eastern front and to near certain death. Von Ebrennac conveys the news on his last night at the farmhouse and, as he prepares to leave, looks at the niece and whispers "Adieu." As he stands motionless at the door, the niece almost wordlessly replies "Adieu," upon which von Ebrennac steps out of the room and their lives. The following morning, von Ebrennac is gone, leaving the uncle and niece to eat their breakfast together in silence.

Yvars, of course, does not manage to reply, even wordlessly, "Goodnight" to Lassalle. Yet his reflex—"they should have called to him, [but] the door was already closing"— though it arrives too late, matches the niece's. In the case of the niece, the silence edges ever so slightly into language, while for Yvars, the language remains just this side of silence. Moreover, the story does not end there. Yvars pedals back home on his bicycle, unable to stop thinking about the girl. The story shudders to a stop with Yvars, who is sitting on the terrace, holding his wife's hand and staring out at the sea, blurting out: "Ah, that's the trouble."[43] We neither see what he sees, nor hear what he hears, but the line cuts to the fundamental obscurity of our lives. In the end, the trouble may be the simple and tragic impossibility of speaking across lives and the predicaments specific to each and every one of them.

At the end of January 1956, Camus flew from Paris to Algiers in order to speak at a public conference dedicated to the impossible proposition that peace was still possible between French and Algerians. Held in the heart of the city, the meeting nearly turned into a riot. While a vast crowd of *pied-noir* protesters milled and shouted outside, inside the hall—whose name, *Cercle du progrès,* sagged with irony— Camus tried to make himself heard above the din.

"This meeting had to take place," he announced to the nervous audience of Arabs and French Algerians, "if only to show that an exchange of views remains possible."[44] He reminded everyone of brute historical and demographic facts. In Algeria "there are a million Frenchmen who have been here for a century, millions of Muslims, either Arabs or Berbers, who have been here for centuries, and several other religious communities."[45] Yet extremists were trying to murder this reality by terrorizing not just the other side but also the moderate members of their own particular groups. If both sides did not open a dialogue, the Frenchman would make up his mind "to know nothing about the Arab, even though he senses within himself that the Arab's demand for dignity is justified, and the Arab makes up his mind to know nothing of the Frenchman, even though he also feels, that the Algerian French likewise has a right to security and dignity on our shared soil."[46] If each and every Frenchman and Muslim did not make an honest "effort to think over his adversary's motives," the violent would carry Algeria away.

By the time he returned to Paris, Camus knew the violent would do precisely that. The organizers had abruptly ended the meeting after Camus finished reading his text: rocks were bursting through the windows and the police cordon outside was on the verge of snapping. What hope was there when the very people who would be protected by Camus' plea for a civilian truce shouted it down and attempted to storm the hall?

Shortly after his return from Algeria, confronted by mounting hostility from both sides and the collapse of his proposal for a civilian truce, Camus resigned as a columnist from the liberal weekly *L'Express* and fell into a silence over the issue of Algeria. The French government's surrender to the uncompromising claims of the *pied-noir* community buried the liberal hope that the Republic would be equal to itself. As for the burgeoning civil war, it was clear that each side would only claim victory with the utter submission of the other. As he told himself, it was best to say nothing so as not to add "either to Algeria's misery or to inanities already written about the situation."[47] Silence was all Camus had left.

This response satisfied neither his friends nor foes: a truth most famously made in December 1957, when Camus traveled to Stockholm to receive the Nobel Prize in Literature. is remembered today less for his official speech than for a heated exchange the day before the ceremony between Camus and an Algerian student. During a question-and-answer session with Swedish students, the young Algerian began to assail Camus for his silence over Algeria. Repeatedly interrupted in his efforts to reply, Camus finally imposed himself: "Though I have been silent for a year and eight months, that doesn't mean I have stopped acting. I've always been a supporter for a just Algeria in which two equal peoples would live peacefully. I've repeatedly demanded that justice be rendered to the Algerian people and that they be given full democratic rights." The spiral of violence in Algeria, Camus continued, had grown so rapidly that he feared any additional words would only quicken it further. When the student again baited him, Camus brought the confrontation to an end: "I have always condemned terror. But I must also condemn terrorism that strikes blindly, for example in the streets of Algiers, and which might strike my mother and family. I believe in justice, but I'll defend my mother before justice."[48]

This, at least, is the version that has come down to us, thanks to the following day's account in the newspaper *Le Monde*. But Camus' actual reply was, in fact, very different: "People are now planting bombs in the tramways of Algiers. My mother might be on one of those tramways. If *that* is justice, then I prefer my mother." The newspaper, which sympathized with the Algerian nationalists and cordially despised Camus, published the correction

three days later. As with all such corrections, it was con-
signed to immediate obscurity.[49]

Justice, love, silence: this is, intriguingly, the same
combination of ideals found in one of Camus' most debated remarks. One can of course imagine conflicts between the claims of justice, the most public of goods, and
those of love, the most private of values. Yet as his reply to
the Algerian student reveals, Camus refused to accept that
love and justice most often not only coexisted, but that
they were in fact conjoined. For Camus, love and justice
are the entwined ideals that moor us to the world and to
one another. When France, during the last months of the
occupation, fought a different kind of civil war, Camus
affirmed that man must "exalt justice in order to fight
against eternal injustice, create happiness in order to
protest against the universe of unhappiness."[50] Yet in the
Algerian bloodbath, where there was nothing "indiscriminate" or "blind" in the taking of civilian lives—to the
contrary, both sides with great discrimination targeted
civilians in order to sow terror—men and women had
abandoned the duty of remaining faithful to the world,
allowing injustice and unhappiness to reign.

In his letter to *Le Monde,* Camus corrected not only the
paper's misquotation, but also corrected, though indirectly, the reasons given for his silence: "I would also like
to say, in regard to the young Algerian who questioned me,
that I feel closer to him than to many French people who
speak about Algeria without knowing it. He knew what he
was talking about, and his face reflected not hatred but
despair and unhappiness. I share that unhappiness."

Words had proved at best useless, at worst complicit in the widening gyre of violence in Algeria. Just as with his mother, when he felt, silently, an "immense pity spread out around him," so too with the student: "When one keeps quiet, the situation becomes clear."[51] The tragic situation of his native Algeria, Camus realized, called upon him to maintain his quiet.

The temptation is great to speak, or to shout, when others fall silent; whether it is because of simple social embarrassment, or a deeper anguish over what cannot be articulated, it is hard to say. It is also the occasion for commentators to run riot with words to fill the gaps left, either wittingly or not, by their subjects. But we must resist the temptation, if only because Camus himself points us to an answer. In his late essay "Return to Tipasa," written shortly before Algeria went to war with itself, Camus describes his efforts to balance the two great forces in his life "even when they contradict one another": the equally sublime wonder of the world and ethical duties of the individual. "Yes, there is beauty and there are the humiliated. Whatever difficulties the enterprise may present, I would like never to be unfaithful either to one or the other." But, he continues, "this still sounds like ethics, and we live for something that transcends ethics. If we could name it, what silence would follow!"[52]

Camus' silence over the war ravaging his native Algeria, the source of nearly all his images of worldly beauty, did not transcend ethics. Instead, it flowed from his recognition that the humiliated were on both sides in this conflict: the great majority of *pieds-noirs* as well as Arabs.

In essence, the truths at play in Algeria—a place that was not an abstraction, but his very life, the land where his family, his mother, lived—were, for Camus, incompatible. In his Nobel speech, Camus said that silence, at certain moments, "takes on a terrifying sense." Algeria was, for Camus, one of those moments—a tragedy for which further words were worse than useless because, incapable of stemming the catastrophe, they would serve only to obscure its dimensions and meaning.

Camus first discovered Friedrich Nietzsche as a teenager—his university professor and mentor, Jean Grenier, made the introductions—and his first published essay, edited by Grenier and published in the journal *Sud,* was on Nietzsche and music. His lifelong engagement with Nietzsche, admiring but critical, sprawls across his notebooks. "I owe to Nietzsche a part of who I am," he acknowledged, gratefully.[53]

What Camus most admired was Nietzsche's slashing and mordant style, as well as his fierce clarity about a world that no longer supported the religious or metaphysical fictions with which humankind had burdened it. In *The Myth of Sisyphus,* Camus praises Nietzsche for having banished all hope for the future: "Nietzsche appears to be the only artist to have derived the extreme consequence of an aesthetic of the Absurd, inasmuch as his final message lies in a sterile and conquering lucidity and an obstinate negation of any supernatural consolation."[54] Casting himself as the surveyor of the varieties of nihilism flowering in our emptied cosmos, Nietzsche had the courage to call a void a void. Yet, he was a nihilist not by vocation, but by necessity: "He diagnosed in himself, and in others, the inability to believe and the disappearance of the primitive foundation of all faith—namely, the belief in life."[55]

Michel Onfray notes that Camus, a serious reader of Nietzsche, was nevertheless not a Nietzschean.[56] By the time he published *The Myth of Sisyphus,* Camus discovered that Nietzsche had dazzled other readers apart from himself, but with catastrophic consequences. In a world relieved of God and morality, everything was indeed permitted. Under the sun of Algiers, the embrace of fate—Nietzsche's *amor fati,* his Zarathustrian "Yes!" to all joys and all woes—dovetailed with Camus' youthful love of the world. But the iron sky over Auschwitz, Camus insisted, forced us to reconsider the ways in which yet others had interpreted Nietzsche. We know, Camus announced, Nietzsche's "posterity and what kind of politics were to claim the authorization of the man who claimed to be the last antipolitical German. He dreamed of tyrants who were artists. But tyranny comes more naturally than art to mediocre men."[57]

And yet Nietzsche remained with Camus to the end. On January 2, 1960, when the car in which Camus was driving smashed into the plane tree alongside the road, killing both him and the driver, his friend Michel Gallimard, Camus' briefcase was flung several yards from the car. It contained his identity papers, a copy of Shakespeare's *Othello,* the manuscript for *The First Man,* and a copy of *The Gay Science*. In this collection of aphorisms, Nietzsche jousts with Socrates, the philosopher who never wrote, yet at the same time never seemed to be short of words. Not only was Socrates "the wisest chatterer of all time," Nietzsche remarks, "he was equally great in silence." He then laments, ironically, that Socrates failed to be silent when it was most essential: as he died, he uttered his famously elusive remark to his friend Crito: "I owe Asclepius a rooster." For Nietzsche, this meant nothing less than that even Socrates, the most cheerful and courageous of men, nevertheless "suffered life." As a result, Nietzsche concluded: "We must overcome even the Greeks!"[58]

Must we, though? In his notebooks, Camus describes a visit he made in 1954 to Turin. According to the much-told story, it was there that, in 1889, Nietzsche, witnessing a cart-driver whip his failing horse, lunged across the street, threw his arms around the animal and collapsed to the ground. When Franz Overbeck arrived a few days later to care for Nietzsche, the delirious man flung himself, weeping, on the neck of his overwhelmed friend. Nietzsche soon after suffered a stroke; until his death in 1900, he never again spoke. "I can never reread this account," Camus wrote, "without crying."[59] He lingered in front of the apartment building where Overbeck came to see Nietzsche, vainly trying to recreate the scene in his mind. But he would not stop trying: in his study, Camus tacked to the wall a headshot of Nietzsche, given to him by his friend René Char, taken after the author of *Thus Spoke Zarathustra* had slipped into permanent silence.[60]

Erich Heller has eloquently written on Nietzsche's "flow of articulation"—a force field of words fending off what Heller describes as Nietzsche's fear of what cannot be expressed: his epic and inevitably failed effort to "escape from transience, oblivion, the inarticulate."[61] Heller weaves this remarkable portrait with a single thread: a hallucination Nietzsche experienced in which he glimpsed a figure who, unable to speak, instead made a "horrifyingly inarticulate sound." Just as Heller warns that we must be careful of making too much about such remarkable findings, so too must we be careful in Camus' case. Yet there is a stunning echo of Nietzsche's jotting in Camus' notebooks. In the summer of 1956, shortly before the Battle of Algiers erupted, Camus wrote a note for *The First Man:* "Novel's end. Maman. What was her silence saying. What was this mute and smiling mouth screaming. We will be resurrected. Her patience at the airfield, in this world of machines and offices that is beyond her, waiting without a word, as old women have for millennia all over the world, waiting for the world to pass. And then very small, a bit broken, on the immense ground, toward the howling monsters, holding her well-combed hair with one hand."[62]

There is, of course, nothing monstrous in Camus' vision, nor did he seek to escape it. On the contrary, he faithfully circled around it in his fiction and in his life, puzzling over his mother's silence—her inability to articulate her love for her son. Less than a year before his death, Camus flew to Algiers after his mother was hospitalized. While the family sits around her bed, "dense, mute and waiting," the mother "suffers silently." This silence, persistent and profound, not only drove Camus to words, but kept him tethered to the world. After a particularly difficult night during Camus' stay in Algiers, a morning rain washed over the city: "The wisterias: they filled my youth with their scent, with their rich and mysterious ardor ... Again, endlessly. They have been more alive, more present in my life than many people . . . except the one who suffers next to me and whose silence has never ceased speaking to me throughout half my life."[63]

Like his mother, like us, perhaps even like Socrates, Camus suffered life he never believed we needed to overcome.

3

MEASURE

Toward the end of *The Rebel,* following a grim climb up the morally and intellectually blasted slope of postwar Europe, Camus described the perspective he had won:

> Historical absolutism, despite its triumphs, has never ceased to come into collision with an irrepressible demand of human nature, of which the Mediterranean, where intelligence is intimately related to the blinding light of the sun, guards the secret. . . . Thrown into the unworthy melting pot of Europe, deprived of beauty and friendship, we Mediterraneans, the proudest of races, live always by the same light. In the depths of the European night, solar thought, the civilization facing two ways awaits its dawn. But it already illuminates the paths of real mastery.[1]

While Camus' insights into the entwined natures of totalitarianism and communism proved prescient, and
the lyricism of his language provokes admiration, both
one and the other rattled the teeth of contemporary intellectuals. *The Rebel*, as we saw, is mostly remembered
today for the spectacular falling out between Camus and
Jean-Paul Sartre. But Sartre wasn't alone in finding fault
with Camus' essay. There flared a series of barbed ex-
changes between Camus and the founder of surrealism,
André Breton, revealing both the size of the moral stake
and personalities involved. In a chapter titled "The
Poets' Rebellion," Camus lambasted surrealism's attachment to the unconscious and irrational as the guarantee
of human servitude. He also blasted the moral irrespon-
sibility of Breton's notorious phrase, found in the movement's foundational work, *The Second Manifesto of Surrealism,* that seems to urge the reader to dash into a crowd
and fire a pistol as quickly and blindly as possible. An
outraged Breton in turn mocked Camus' effort to marry
revolt and moderation, asking: "Once revolt has been
emptied of its passionate substance, what could possibly
remain?"[2]

The ad hominem violence of the literary exchange tends
to obscure the immense moral and political stakes posed
by *The Rebel.* For Camus, matters were simple: he could no
more accept communism's eschatological promises than
he could submit to our existing condition. In *The Rebel* he
sets out to discover the grounds on which we refuse both
these options and finds them in the absurd nature of our

world—a world in which the Mediterranean is the source of the very trait Sartre and Breton savage: *la mesure.*

In early 1942, Camus jotted in his notebook: "Calypso offers Ulysses a choice between immortality and the land of his birth. He rejects immortality. Therein lies perhaps the whole meaning of the *Odyssey.*"[3] This remains, for Camus, the meaning not just of the *Odyssey,* but of ancient Greece. It is Odysseus's embrace of measure, choosing a life tethered to our world, which frames the ancient Greek worldview. As he wrote nearly two decades later in *The Rebel,* Homer's hero "refuses divinity in order to share the struggles and the destiny of every man." Like Odysseus, Camus declares, we must "choose the faithful land of Ithaka . . . Bathed in light, the world remains our first and last love."[4]

Camus thus merges the nostalgia of Odysseus—his twenty-year *nostos,* or effort to return home—with his own deeply felt homesickness. Camus' longing was not only physical—for the land and water, blue sky and bright light of his native Algeria—but also metaphysical: a yearning for a meaning or a unity to our lives, one which he felt most deeply as a child growing up in Algiers. These entwined senses of loss surge not just across the pages of *The Rebel,* but across all of Camus' writings, from his earlier essays to his last and unfinished work, *The First Man.*

But nostalgia is a complicated matter. By the time Odysseus swears his fidelity to Ithaka, he has lost all of his shipmates, witnessed acts of stunning barbarity, traveled to the underworld and back, and slept with a number of minor goddesses. Moreover, he learns that Ithaka has been invaded and colonized by a mob of suitors who are gorging themselves on the riches of his palace while competing for Penelope's hand. Odysseus will, of course, slaughter all of the suitors—including those, Homer tells us, who do not merit this death—leading Ithaka to the edge of civil war. It is only the intervention of Athena, who makes the warring side *forget* the reasons for their rage, which imposes peace on this rocky island afloat in the Mediterranean.

Camus does not note these details, yet they deeply resonate with his own life as a faithful son of both ancient Greece and modern Algeria. Greek myth allowed Camus to give expression to this dual fidelity. If, as he wrote, "the world of myth wherein I feel most at home is the world of Greek myth," this world encompassed the southern shores of the Mediterranean.[5] In fact, Camus mines several of these myths not only to make sense of his life, but also to make sense of our lives. Whether in the case of a war-torn Algeria or a meaning-shorn cosmos, Camus turns to the Greeks as guides to lead him from his perplexity.

The classicist Ulrich von Wilamowitz once affirmed: "To make the ancients speak, we must feed them with our own blood."[6] In similar terms, Camus declared: "Myths have no life of their own. They wait for us to give them flesh."[7] And once given flesh, myths grow and evolve. Soon after the publication of *The Myth of Sisyphus* in 1942,

Camus concluded that he had to move beyond the absurd. While an accurate diagnosis of the human condition, he knew it was not a guide to France's desperate predicament as a nation subjected to Nazi rule. By the time
he had joined the Resistance, eventually becoming the editor of the clandestine paper *Combat,* Camus was already
looking ahead to a second cycle of works devoted to the
theme of rebellion. This changed focus led to *The Plague,
The Just Assassins,* and *The Rebel:* a new set of triplets that
Camus baptized with the name of Prometheus.

As we saw in the preceding chapter, Camus' interest in
Prometheus went back even further than it did with Sisyphus. In 1937, he adapted Paul Mazon's French translation of Aeschylus's *Prometheus Bound* for the theatrical
company, the *Théâtre du travail,* he had founded with
friends. It was in this same period that Camus joined the
Communist Party: drama, for the young *pied-noir,* was an
ideal means to reach and educate the working class. In
a manifesto penned by Camus, the company declared its
intent "to demonstrate that it is sometimes advantageous
to art to descend from its ivory tower ... [and] restore some
human values."[8]

In this cause, Camus found an ideal ally in Prometheus.
Yet, as with Sisyphus, Aeschylus's Prometheus is just one
among many variations of the mythic figure. For example,
in his *Theogony,* Hesiod presents a Prometheus who is not
terribly different from Sisyphus: a fast-talking Titan who
repeatedly scams Zeus. Prometheus's decision to give
humankind the gift of fire—the act for which Zeus chains
him to a pillar, with an eagle feasting daily on his liver—
seems less his goal than to goad Zeus.

The hero of *Prometheus Bound,* however, is equal to the austere and terrifying tragedy conceived by Aeschylus. The only extant play of a presumed trilogy, *Prometheus Bound* ends with the chained hero who refuses to submit to Zeus. Prometheus tells Hermes, Zeus's messenger, that no torture will break him: "There's no outrageous treatment, no device/By which Zeus will induce me to tell these things/Until the indignity of these chains is undone." For Camus, a militant leftist appalled by the condition of Arabs no less than the working poor of the *pied-noir* community, this accidental ending—based on fragmentary evidence, the trilogy ends with Zeus freeing Prometheus—made perfect sense. Less than a year after the play's production, Camus further embraced a Prometheus marked by revolutionary verve: "The spirit of revolution lies wholly in man's protest against the human condition. Under the different forms that it assumes, it is . . . the only eternal theme of art and religion. A revolution is always carried out against the Gods—from that of Prometheus onwards."[9]

But this sentiment of revolutionary élan, the extreme gesture of rebelling against the gods and the order they enshrined, also appealed to a youthful and ambitious artist thoroughly captivated by the physical beauty of his country. In his notebook, less than a year after the production of *Prometheus Unbound,* Camus exhorted himself to "find excess in moderation."[10] So, too, in his essay "Nuptials at Tipasa," written in 1936, Camus offers a paean to sensual excess: "We walk toward an encounter with love and desire. We are not seeking lessons or the bitter philosophy one requires of greatness. Everything seems futile here except the sun, our kisses, and the wild scents of the earth. . . . Here, I leave order and moderation to others."[11] Yet more emphatically, Tipasa, this gateway to antiquity, makes him understand "what is meant by glory: the right to love without limits."[12]

Tragedy, for Camus, was a constituent element to what he called "la pensée de midi," the worldview he associated with the Mediterranean. The same year his theater company staged *Prometheus Bound,* Camus gave a public talk, titled "The New Mediterranean Culture," at the Maison de la Culture in Algiers. In it, Camus sketched his conception of "Mediterraneanism," a movement founded in the interwar period by the Algerian writer Gabriel Audisio, which sought to reclaim the "spirit of the Mediterranean" from the Italian Fascists and their idolization of Rome and instead place it under the humanistic aegis of ancient Greece.[13]

Yet what Camus understood by the "Mediterranean" did not always match the cartographic reality of the region. In a section of his lecture titled "Evidences," or "Obvious Facts," he offers not a fact, but a factoid: "There is a Mediterranean sea, a basin linking about ten different countries." In each of these countries you find the same "appreciation of life" among "casually dressed men" who live "the violent, colorful life we all know."[14]

Except, perhaps, if you are a casually dressed man, or woman, from parts of North Africa or the Middle East. In 1937, there were not ten, but fifteen countries bordering the Mediterranean. In his math, Camus seems bound to the privileged perspective of Europe. Egypt and the

eastern Mediterranean littoral are entirely ignored, while
the two "Arab" countries he does name, Algeria and Tu-
nisia, were both under French rule. Moreover, while he
discussed the origins and evolution of Christianity and
Judaism, Camus did not have a word to say about Islam.
Finally, when Camus did make mention of "Arabs," the
questions multiply rather than disappear. North Africa, he
declared, "is one of the few countries where East and West
live close together. And there is, at this junction, little difference between the way a Spaniard or an Italian lives on
the quays of Algiers, and the way Arabs live around them."
Even when one takes into account the stratified nature of
pied-noir society, one that encompassed wealthy colons as
well as dirt-poor laborers like Camus' own family, there remained a dizzying abyss between the economic, legal, and
social conditions of the European settlers in Algeria and
the indigenous Arab and Berber communities.

Not surprisingly, one of Camus' most powerful antico-
lonialist critics, Conor Cruise O'Brien, concluded that
this advocate of a new Mediterranean culture "reveals
himself as incapable of thinking in any categories other
than those of a Frenchman."[15] But as Neil Foxlee has recently argued, Camus' effort to forge a new Mediterranean identity—in other words, inventing a myth equal to
the challenge of his time—was not an effort to evade the
reality of colonialism, but to address its shortcomings.[16]
The context, in this case, is as important as the text itself.
The Communist Party of Algeria, the only party that
demanded full civil and political rights for the Arab
and Berber populations, had created the Maison de la

Culture. This platform inspired Camus' (short-lived) membership in the party, as well as his even earlier participation, when still at lycée, in a journal called *Ikdam*. Founded by the grandson of the nineteenth-century Algerian nationalist Abd al-Kadir, the journal called upon France to extend the rights of man and citizen to the Arabs and Berbers under its rule.[17]

In the same year he announced the birth of a new Mediterranean culture, Camus joined the staff of the independent newspaper *Alger républicain*. He quickly graduated from writing on *fait divers* to investigative reports, the most striking of which was his series of reports from the eastern region of Kabylia in 1939. Tellingly, the first of these dispatches was titled "*Grèce en haillons*," or "Greece in Rags." The piece fuses Camus' nostalgia for ancient Greece with outrage over conditions in modern Algeria: "When one reaches the first slopes of Kabylia, catching sight of small villages huddled near the summits, the men draped in white woolen robes, the paths bordered by olive trees, fig trees and cactus, the simplicity of life and landscape, man and earth, one cannot help but think of Greece."[18]

That is, until one gets closer, whereupon the ideal of ancient Greece collapsed under the brutal reality of everyday life in Kabylia. For example, it was public knowledge that the official distribution of grain did not meet the needs of the population. But, as Camus writes, "what I did not know is that these shortages were killing people."[19] He goes on to depict the horrifying reality of villages where malnourished children played by open sewers, fainted from hunger in classrooms, fought with dogs over kitchen scraps, were wracked by convulsions and died from eating poisonous roots. The wretchedness of everyday life gave the lie to the excuse of imperial apologists—namely, that the Berber "mentality" was the source of these ills. Nonsense, replied Camus. It was a question of water, food, roads, and schools—all of which Kabylia sorely lacked and the French authorities did not supply. Camus dispatched a dozen articles from Kabylia, all of which carried the same message: the misery of these human beings must not be obscured by "glib phrases or meditations. It cries for our attention, it despairs of getting it."[20]

Seen through the prism of subsequent events, one might conclude that the stance taken by Camus—as a staff member of *Ikdam* or reporter for *Alger républicain*—was simply naive. Perhaps. But such naiveté retained a moral cogency in the interwar period. Camus belonged to a small number of French Algerians who believed, in good faith, that the official republican policy of assimilation, rather than a cloak for the brutal reality of colonization, was a blueprint for a fully integrated nation.[21] French colonial policy was, of course, racist and paternalist. Yet, informed by the universal and egalitarian sentiments of 1789, France's republican credo also retained the power to inspire exceptional individuals like Camus to work toward an Algeria that would be fully French, fully republican, and fully free for all of its inhabitants.

It was through the figure of Prometheus that Camus continued to explore the questions of freedom and responsibility. After World War II, as what seemed an eternal winter was settling over Europe, Camus published in 1947 his "Prometheus in the Underworld." A short and lyrical essay, it begins by asking what Prometheus could possibly mean to a world emerging from a world war, freed from the Nazi threat, but now held hostage by the forces of communism and capitalism. In his reply, Camus now straddles the political and metaphysical, physical and spiritual worlds: "Prometheus was the hero who loved men enough to give them fire and liberty, technology and art. Today, mankind needs and cares only for technology. We rebel through our machines, holding art and what art implies as an obstacle and a symbol of slavery. But what characterizes Prometheus is that he cannot separate machines from art."[22]

Had this same Prometheus, so hated by Zeus, appeared amid the rubble of postwar Europe, the era's great technological and ideological actors would also have hauled him away: "They would nail him to a rock, in the name of the very humanism he was the first to symbolize."[23] Those who have chosen "history"—those who had embraced the millenarian vision offered by communism—have betrayed Prometheus's legacy: "this son 'both bold in thought and light of heart.'"[24] While Prometheus is a rebel with a cause—or, more precisely, causes—it is on Prometheus's heroic gesture, his act of rebellion against Zeus's reign, that Camus continues to dwell. At the end of *Prometheus Bound,* we are left with a god who, refusing to recant his challenge to the established order, suffers unspeakable torment. His final line—"Look on me, how unjustly I suffer!"—echoes the romantic defiance of fate so attractive to the young Camus.

It was at this same moment that Camus became an editor at Gallimard, where he launched a series titled *"Espoir."* Undoubtedly, his most important discovery as editor was the work of Simone Weil. The radical political theorist, philosopher, and religious mystic died in relative obscurity in England in 1943, where she had gone two years earlier in order to join General de Gaulle's Free French movement. Apart from a few scattered articles and essays, nearly all of Weil's writing was still unpublished. Over the next several years, in collaboration with Weil's family, Camus edited and published several of Weil's works, ranging from her political essays, most notably *L'Enracinement,* to religious works such as *La Connaissance surnaturelle.*

But perhaps the most important convergence between Camus and Weil was on the subject of ancient Greece. In 1953, he published Weil's *La Source grecque,* a collection of essays on Greek antiquity. Most notably, the collection contained the seminal essay "The Iliad, or the Poem of Force" as well as an introduction to the thought of Heraclitus.

It is difficult to measure Weil's influence on Camus. At his press conference in Stockholm in 1958, the Nobel Prize winner tellingly cited just two French writers with whom he felt close: the poet and close friend René Char and Weil.[25] His biographer Olivier Todd notes that Camus was "fascinated" by Weil, but he disliked her "penchant for misery and death."[26] That fascination was, in part, political: Camus considered the analysis of human needs and duties in *L'Enracinement* to be a revelation.[27] But Camus found Weil's treatment of ancient Greece no less revelatory. He was, no doubt, particularly taken by Weil's discussion of "force" in the Homeric epics and Aeschylean tragedies. For Weil, force is a brute fact universal in its reach and consistent in its consequences. Indiscriminate and ineluctable, force levels the strong and weak, transforming victim and victimizer into "things." As Weil writes, "Force is as pitiless to the man who possesses it, or thinks he does, as it is to its victims; the second it crushes, the first it intoxicates. The truth is, nobody really possesses it."[28]

Yet those in power consistently abuse their authority, unaware that their mastery of force is utterly illusory. Retribution inevitably arrives—the means by which the gods reestablish a divine equilibrium. This form of rebalancing or reckoning, for Weil, "was the main subject of Greek thought. It is the soul of the epic ... [and] it functions as the mainspring of Aeschylus's tragedies."[29] She then notes that we have lost this conception of limit—indeed, the West no longer even has "a word to express it in any of its languages: conceptions of limit, measure, equilibrium, which ought to determine the conduct of life are, in the West, restricted to a servile function in the vocabulary of technics. We are only geometricians of matter; the Greeks were, first of all, geometricians in their apprenticeship to virtue."[30]

The works of the Promethean cycle, in particular *The Plague* and *The Rebel*, reflect Weil's austere, yet nuanced understanding of the cosmos. Camus recreates, in the heart of the twentieth century, the mystery he had discovered in Aeschylean tragedy and recasts in light of Weil's work. It is a universe where both Prometheus and Zeus are right, but neither is justified, a universe where the gods impose the impossible choice on Agamemnon of either sacrificing his daughter or abandoning his effort to retrieve Helen and Greek honor. In a word, it is a universe where human beings are subject to what Bernard Williams calls "supernatural necessity."[31] Or, as the hero of *The Plague*, Dr. Rieux, confesses when asked against whom or what he is fighting: "I haven't a notion . . . I assure you I haven't a notion."[32]

Camus must have found Weil's tragic conception of force particularly apt for the immediate postwar era in French Algeria. In mid-1945, he returned to his native land for the first time in nearly three years. During most of April, he crisscrossed the country, braving the growing rumors of violence, gauging the impact that the war had upon relations between the *pied-noir* and Arab and Berber populations. Scarcely had he returned to Paris when the horrifying seesaw massacres in the town of Sétif, begun in frenzy by the Arab population and ended more systematically by French forces, exploded on May 8.

Below the bold headline "Crisis in Algeria," his first article appeared in the May 13 edition of *Combat*, the resistance paper for which Camus had become editor during the war. Warning of the "grave difficulties with which Algeria is grappling today," Camus revealed that little had changed in the conditions of the rural population since his earlier trip to Kabylia: too little food for too many mouths, too many republican ideals given the lie by selfish *pieds-noirs* and feckless French administrators. The people who suffered from these policies "are not inferior except in regard to the conditions in which they must live," but also those who "have spent the past two years fighting for the liberation of France." France's duty was clear: it had to "quell the cruelest of hungers and heal inflamed hearts."[33]

Camus insisted upon the universal quality of human dignity, all the while holding on to the particularity of individual human beings. All French Algerians were duty-bound to "understand [the Algerian Muslims] before we judge them."[34] France, Camus announced, would have to "conquer Algeria a second time."[35] Camus' provocative declaration underscored a prosaic truth: the ideals of the republic extended no further than the European havens in Algeria. If Algeria were to remain part of France, France had to reconquer it not by force of arms, but instead by the systematic and sincere application of the rights, duties, and benefits of citizenship. In his final editorial, Camus declared: "Our feverish and unbridled desire for power and expansion will never be excused unless we make up for them by unwavering attention to the pursuit of justice and the spirit of self-sacrifice. Despite the repressive actions we have just taken in North Africa,

I am convinced that the era of Western imperialism is over."[36]

Camus grasped far better than most of his contemporaries that *Combat*'s slogan, "From Resistance to Revolution," had inspired not just men and women living under the Nazi occupation, but also men and women living under French colonial rule. The French civilizing mission could only be fulfilled, he announced, by bringing "more complete liberation to everyone it subjugates." If France failed to do so, it would "reap hatred like all vanquishers who prove themselves incapable of moving beyond victory." Camus' warning not to repeat the very experience France underwent under the Nazi occupation was remarkable: few on the Left, much less the Right, cast French actions in such terms. More remarkable, however, was his call for justice, despite the blood that had just been shed. "Unfortunate and innocent French victims have lost their lives, and this crime in itself is inexcusable. But I hope that we will respond to murder with nothing other than justice, so as to avoid doing irreparable harm."[37]

Camus' hope was stillborn. In 1955, as the bloodshed mounted in Algeria, Camus traveled to Athens to give a talk on the future of tragedy. Whereas he had once seen *Prometheus Bound* as a vehicle for a tormented god, Camus now plumbed a deeper level of meaning to the tragedy. "The forces confronting each other in tragedy are equally legitimate, equally justified," he told his audience:

Prometheus is both just and unjust, and Zeus
who pitilessly oppresses him also has right on
his side. Melodrama could thus be summed up
by saying: "Only one side is just and justifiable,"
while the perfect tragic formula would be: "All
can be justified, no one is just." This is why the
chorus in classical tragedies generally advises
prudence. For the chorus knows that up to a
certain limit everyone is right and that the person who, from blindness or passion, oversteps
this limit is heading for catastrophe if he persists in his desire to assert a right he thinks he
alone possesses.[38]

From the perspective of the god chained to his pillar—a
heroic and absurd figure—Camus now steps back. Had he
been content to portray Prometheus as the only justified
party, Aeschylus would have written a simple drama indifferent to the vast stakes involved. But his Prometheus
is, all too tragically, both right and wrong: he is right to
give fire to man, yet that same act violates a cosmic order,
or balance, overseen by Zeus. The central concern of classical tragedy, Camus realized, is that limit "must not be
transgressed. On either side of this limit equally legitimate forces meet in quivering and endless confrontation.
To make a mistake about this limit, to try to destroy the
balance, is to perish."[39]

Like Aeschylus's Athena, who at the end of the *Oresteia*
urges the Furies to surrender their desire for vengeance
and avoid any action that "strikes a note of brutal

conquest," Camus asked that all men embrace justice
and, as Athena pleaded, "revere the Mean." At the same
time, his account of Prometheus also grows, now stretch-
ing to contain more than the fire-giver's suffering; there
is also Zeus's right to impose that suffering.

This recasting of the Promethean myth reflects Camus' tragic understanding of strife-torn Algeria. Both
French and Arab communities had equally compelling
claims on the land, both had violated the just expectations of the other, and both sides confronted one another
on a stage where all could be justified, and no one is just.
As the carnage and chaos intensified in Algeria, Camus
worked to persuade the two sides to agree to a civilian
truce. In his "Appeal for a Civilian Truce," announced in
January 1956, a few months after his Greece trip, he demanded that both sides denounce the violence aimed at
all civilians. To his fellow *pieds-noirs,* he urged them to
"recognize what is just in your adversary's cause, as well
as recognize what is not just in their own repressive mea-
sures." And to the National Liberation Front (FLN), he
made the very same demand: "Disavow the murdering of
innocent lives." Before the situation became yet more catastrophic, both sides had to agree to spare civilians. "We
must all demand a truce—a truce that will allow us to
arrive at solutions, a truce regarding the massacre of civilians by both sides."[40]

As Philippe Vanney has recently suggested, a truce is the
legal expression of the mean, at least at times of war.[41]

Inevitably, perhaps, French Algeria was no more able to act on this exhortation than was ancient Athens. Perhaps no less inevitably, Camus eventually withdrew from the public arena, refusing to speak again on what he called his "personal tragedy."[42] In 1960, when he died in a car crash in southern France, his silence suddenly became his final public position on Algeria. It is a silence in which echoes the fate of political and philosophical moderation.

As a political value or philosophical concept, moderation is notoriously elusive. Is it, in fact, a full-bodied theory or worldview? Or, instead, is it little more than a personality trait? Is there, moreover, something questionable about the very desirability of moderation? It is not always the case, after all, that one of the extremes that define a mean is wrong. Or, for that matter, the mean is not always the most desirable end. Ultimately, is it something more than a disposition to avoid extremes, whether or not one of those extremes is desirable?

In a recent work, the political theorist Aurelian Craiutu insists that moderation is a positive theory, one based on the intrinsic values of pluralism, gradualism, and toleration. A moderate, Craiutu suggests, is a thinker who embraces "fallibilism as a middle way between radical skepticism and epistemological absolutism, and acknowledge[s] the limits of political action and the imperfection of the human condition."[43]

Most discussions of ethical or philosophical moderation find their source in Aristotle, particularly his *Nicomachean Ethics*. For the Greek thinker, "excess and deficiency are characteristic of vice" while "the mean is virtue." The mean, however, is not a theoretical or abstract ideal, but a state reached through practice and experience. There is, for Aristotle, no science of the mean; instead, there is only the never-ending series of efforts to reach this state. Inevitably, the individual seeking the mean will at times sin by excess or prudence. This is only natural, Aristotle reassures, for "so shall we most easily hit the mean and what is right."[44]

Remarkably for someone who claimed to be so deeply influenced by ancient Greek thought, Camus never cites Aristotle's *locus classicus* on the subject of moderation. This is not surprising, however: Camus insisted repeatedly that he was not a philosopher.[45] At the very least, it was certainly true that he was not a systematic reader of ancient philosophy. As Paul Archambault justly observes, "Nothing seems to indicate that Camus had anything but a passing acquaintance with Greek thought between the death of Plato and the Christian era."[46]

Camus instead fastened onto Aeschylus and Sopho-cles. (Perhaps influenced by his reading of Nietzsche's *Birth of Tragedy*, Camus had a low opinion of Euripides, dismissing his "rationalist" approach to human drama.) Of course, neither the *Oresteia* nor Oedipus plays offers a fully consistent or cogent "philosophy." The Greek trage-dians were, in this regard, no more "philosophers" than Camus was. But their work is nevertheless philosophical in a different sense of the word: works of art that explore the human condition with a degree of nuance and rich-ness that traditional philosophical systems cannot. As Martha Nussbaum has argued, when we read philosophers like Plato or Kant, our "natural response is that this is not how it *feels* to be in that situation. It does not feel like solving a puzzle, where all that is needed is to find the right answer."[47]

Ever since Plato, an important tradition in moral philosophy is based on the conviction that the proper understanding of the good dictates what we ought to do in a given situation. In other words, that there is one and just one right choice to make. Greek tragedy reveals the emotional poverty of such arguments. It reminds us that our instinctual response to certain moral dilemmas "is connected with other valuable elements of human ethical life—that we would risk giving up something of real importance" if we were to accept, say, a Platonic or Kantian approach.[48] Neither Aeschylus nor Sophocles, Nussbaum contends, offers a solution to certain moral dilemmas for the simple reason that one does not exist. Instead, they portray the problem in all of its terrifying complexity—one that depicts the collision of incommensurable truths. As for the tragic hero, all we can do is allow him "to have his suffering, the natural expression of his goodness of character, and not to stifle these responses out of misguided optimism." And all the Chorus or, indeed, all we can do "is to respect the gravity of his predicament, to respect the responses that express his goodness, and to think about his case as showing a possibility for human life in general."[49]

Nussbaum's words bear directly on Camus' ties to ancient Greek and modern Algerian tragedies. For Camus, the tragic poets speak to our present condition with unparalleled urgency and comprehension. In their depiction of conflicts where each side has an equally valid ethical claim, but in which neither side has the will or desire to recognize the humanity of its opponent, much less the capacity to maintain their measure or sense of proportion, Aeschylus and Sophocles anticipate the tragedy that swept Camus' Algeria. Perhaps the most apposite and appalling rehearsal for the Algerian war for independence, yet one Camus never discussed at length, is Aeschlyus's *Seven Against Thebes,* which recounts the mortal combat for the throne of Thebes between the brothers Eteocles and Polynices. Both men have equally legitimate claim to rule the city; both men are blind to the justice of their sibling's demand. They duel outside the gate of the city; killing one another, the brothers fall into a tangled heap. Yet the city, rather than uniting over this tragedy, carries it forward: as the play concludes, the chorus splits, as one half follows Ismene and the corpse of Eteocles, and the other half follows Antigone and the body of Polynices. As Antigone cries: "Last of the gods, the Fury, sower of discord/Has still the last word."[50]

Two and a half millennia stand between between Aeschylus's Thebes and Camus' Algeria, yet they are terrifyingly close. As Camus understood, tragedy alone could reflect French Algeria's predicament, as well as his own. Like the Greek chorus, he was torn in half by the conflict. He knew that the claims of each side in Algeria were, like those at ancient Thebes, equally just. The problem, of course, is that the actors both then and in Camus' own time were incapable of seeing any side or claim but their own. Eteocles, for example, forgets that his brother has an equally valid claim to the throne. The terrorists of the Organisation de l'armée secrete (OAS), just like the terrorists of the FLN, were no less blind and bloodthirsty. Like Agamemnon, who in Aeschylus's *Oresteia* transforms his daughter Iphigenia into a sacrificial animal in order to pursue his invasion of Troy, both sides in the Algerian tragedy not only slit one another's throats but also the throats of innocents in their own camps.

In his grim postmortem of Algeria's war of independence, Ferhat Abbas, the leader of moderate Algerian nationalists, wrote: "We had been victims of a myth. In their turn, the *pieds-noirs* had been victims of a long mystification. They had been told for more than a century that Algeria, a French department, was only the prolongation of metropolitan France. They believed it. When the hour of truth rang, for them as for us they felt betrayed. Thus, they fought bitterly to make this aberrant fiction last."[51] Abbas's justifiably bitter reflection on the myth of French Algeria is telling. The promise of political and civil equality held out to the Arabs and Berbers of Algeria proved to be as mythical as the French conceit that Algeria was part and parcel of France. And the fiction was certainly "aberrant" when proclaimed by defenders of the status quo, not to mention supporters of the OAS, in French Algeria.

Yet Abbas's assessment does not make room for the more complex attitude of individuals like Camus, a *pied-noir* whom he long admired. While Camus had mythologized

Algeria, casting it in the tradition of Greek measure, he neither subjected it nor was subject to ideological or political "mystification." Camus was not deceived by the desperate inequalities that harrowed his native land—inequalities he never tired of denouncing. Yet, by the end of his life, Camus understood that his warnings, perhaps like Cassandra's, had fallen on uncomprehending ears. In effect, his position on Algeria had returned to the world of Aeschylean tragedy. Just like the ancient trilogy, history for Camus finally stopped at *Prometheus Bound:* he could not go beyond the first play. Its conclusion, with Prometheus's cry that he was the unhappiest of the gods, rehearsed the cry of both French and Arab Algerians in the 1950s. Camus' later interpretation of the play—at its core, a plea for limits—reflected in his call for a civilian truce, failed to find an audience. This was perhaps less because Camus was too idealistic in this effort, than that it was too premature: France and Algeria had scarcely written the first play of their own tragedy in the Mediterranean. Several more years were necessary for the two subsequent plays to be written.

The Greeks, Camus insisted, are never vindictive: "In their most audacious flights they always remain faithful to the idea of moderation, a concept they deified."[52] But they were no less faithful to the idea of tragic situations: those moments in life and art that are immune to resolution. As Nussbaum underscores, tragedy *teaches:* "There is a kind of knowing that works by suffering because suffering is the appropriate acknowledgement of the way human life, in these cases, is."[53] In his effort to make sense of French Algeria's predicament through the works of Greek tragedy, Camus' work reminds us that, as the Chorus in the Oresteia sings: "Through suffering comes knowledge."

4

FIDELITY

A man wakes before dawn, dresses quietly so as not to disturb his wife, and rides into town to watch a man be put to death. It was neither fascination nor bloodlust that pushed the man to attend the public execution, but instead a sense of outraged justice: the criminal had, in a murderous frenzy, bludgeoned to death not just a husband and wife on their farm, but their children as well. When the husband returned to the house after the execution, he rushed past his wife, vomited in the bathroom, and collapsed in bed. Until the end of his life the man refused to speak about what he saw that day.

Most readers of Camus will recognize this story about his father, Lucien Camus. It surfaces intact in his first and last novels, *The Stranger* and *The First Man*, as well as in his long essay "Reflections on the Guillotine," and floats to the surface of *The Plague* in bits and pieces. In fact, this story—one of the few Camus' mother was able to tell about her husband—haunts the near entirety of Camus' writings.

In *The First Man,* the hero Jacques Cormery, seeking news about the dead father he never knew, hears a similar story recounted by his school principal, Monsieur Levesque. Several years earlier, Levesque and Cormery *père* had served together as French soldiers in Morocco. Stationed in the Atlas Mountains, they were ordered to relieve their comrades from their shift at an advance post. When they reached the position, they found that the rebels had slit the throats of their comrades, and stuffed their genitals into their mouths.

Once they returned to camp, Cormery suddenly exploded: "A man doesn't let himself do that kind of thing! That's what makes a man, or otherwise. . . . I'm poor, I came from an orphanage, they put me in this uniform, they dragged me into the war, but I wouldn't let myself do that." When Levesque reminded his companion that Frenchmen had committed equally horrific crimes, Cormery shot back: "Then they too, they aren't men." He then cried out: "A filthy race! What a race! All of them, all of them . . ." And just as Lucien Camus took refuge into his bedroom upon returning home from the public execution, Cormery, "white as a sheet, went into his tent."[1]

The "dread that so distressed his father" had been left to his son as "his only clear and certain legacy."[2] Indeed, the dread was the fruit of a conviction with roots as deep as the grape vines that Lucien Camus tended as a vineyard foreman. Camus' loyalty to the visceral ethics expressed by his father—the intuitive conviction that humankind, if it wishes to preserve this status, must obey certain limits on its freedom, all the while acknowledging the humanity of one's fellow men and women—endured his entire life. It was an ethics based on faithfulness to our fundamental duties and faithfulness to our world. For Camus, it was the same fidelity revealed by his father upon seeing the ritualistic dismemberment by Arab terrorists of French soldiers, and in a French prison to the equally ritualistic act of a "quivering body dropped onto a board to have its head cut off."[3]

Fidelity, the philosopher André Comte-Sponville has claimed, is not one virtue among others; it is, instead, the one virtue that makes the others possible.[4] For example, would justice be worth anything at all if the world was empty of people faithful to that virtue? Or what value could we ever find in peace without the presence of peacemakers committed to that ideal? And would not truth itself wither if there were not individuals who insisted on telling truth to power?

But we must be careful: fidelity's value can be weighed only by first weighing the object toward which it flows. As Vladimir Jankélévitch concludes, "Faithfulness to stupidity is yet one more stupidity."[5] Fidelity to one's political party at the cost of loyalty to one's humanity is not fidelity, but most often betrayal. The vow of loyalty signed by French bureaucrats to Marshal Pétain leads us from the realm of virtue to that of evil. This becomes yet clearer with the SS vow of loyalty to Hitler. In an interview,

Camus cites this very example when he notes "fidelity is not, in itself, a virtue."[6]

By the same token, fidelity to nihilism is unworthy of the name. In the maelstrom of a world war incited by the ideological nihilism embodied by Nazi Germany, Fascist Italy, and Communist Russia, Camus wrote a series of four "letters" to a fictitious German friend. Published in resistance journals during the last two years of the war, "Letters to a German Friend" explores the two primordial and fatally opposed responses to a world without meaning. As Camus announces in the first letter: "We are fighting for the distinction between sacrifice and mysticism, between energy and violence, between strength and cruelty, for that even finer distinction between the true and the false."[7]

Fidelity begins with the recognition that this distinction is not just meaningful, but with the knowledge that strength, sacrifice, and energy must serve the demands of the most fundamental of truths: the outrage of a meaningless cosmos impels all of humankind to struggle against it. Herein laid the difference between Camus and his German friend: "Simply that you readily accepted despair and I never yielded to it. Simply that you saw the injustice of our condition to the point of being willing to add to it, whereas it seemed to me that man must exalt justice in order to fight against injustice, create happiness in order to protest against the universe of unhappiness." While the German, convinced there was no alternative, flew into the embrace of nihilism, Camus "merely wanted men to rediscover their solidarity in order to wage war against their revolting fate."[8]

This revolting fate was, all too often, the work of men under the sway of nihilism. In the months leading to the Allied landings, the German forces, abetted by *la milice,* the French paramilitary units that collaborated in the bloody repression, waged war on France's civilian population. In "For Three Hours They Shot Frenchmen," Camus documents the murder of eighty-six men in the town of Ascq. With great concision, he narrates the actions of the Germans, from the moment they "fired on three prostrate employees [at the train station]" to the sixty men "who were rounded up to a pasture" and shot. Camus then turns to the reader: "Eighty-six men just like you, the readers of this newspaper, passed before the German guns. Eighty-six men: enough to fill three or four rooms the size of the room you're sitting in. Eighty-six faces, drawn or defiant, eighty-six faces overwhelmed by horror or by hatred." Dwelling on the unrelenting length of the slaughter, Camus offers another everyday reference: "Three hours, the amount of time that some of you will have spent that day at dinner or talking quietly with friends, while elsewhere people watched a film and laughed at made-up adventures. For three hours, minute after minute, without a letup, without a pause, in a single French village, shots were fired one after another and bodies fell writhing to the ground."[9]

Or the amount of time it took to read this book to this point. The article's immediate aim, of course, is justice: to gather evidence to be used against the Germans and their French collaborators once France was liberated.

But, more broadly, the goal of Camus' exercise in the phenomenology of evil is "so that nothing be forgotten."[10] At the end of the day—and end of our lives—we must be faithful, insofar as it is humanly possible, to our past, as it was lived and understood by contemporaries, and not to falsehoods generated by governments or images d'Epinal offered by the press. We must avoid caricatures and captious versions of the past; indeed, fidelity, Jankélévitch writes, "is the virtue of memory, and memory itself is a virtue." The past, unlike the present or future, cannot defend itself: we alone can protect it against the tendencies to forget, traduce or—which amounts to more or less the same thing—transform it.[11]

In his fourth and final letter, Camus tells his German friend that he will resist and defeat him, but that he refuses to hate him: "Despite all the tortures inflicted on our people, despite our disfigured dead and our villages peopled with orphans, I can tell you that at the very moment when we are going to destroy you without pity, we still feel no hatred for you."[12] While this claim may strike us as mere posturing, it is of a piece with the ethics of fidelity. Resentment, after all, is fidelity to an unworthy emotion: hatred or anger. As such, it has no place in an ethics that insists the ends can never justify the means—and no less important, the means are at times justified only by their ends. Several years later, in an interview, Camus echoed Jankélévitch's insistence that what we must seek "is not any and all sorts of fidelity, but instead good and great faithfulness."[13] When asked whether faithfulness can justify a life, Camus replied it could and must—*if* the faithfulness served life and happiness, not death and servitude. "Undoubtedly, one of the last questions a man can ask about the value of his life is 'Have I been faithful?' But this question means nothing if it does not first of all mean 'Have I done nothing to degrade my life or another's?'"[14]

Toward the end of 1941, when still in Oran, living with his wife Francine in an apartment owned by her parents, Camus noted in his journal that great works of art are often made in times of great historical turmoil. He cites as examples Shakespeare and Milton, Rabelais and Montaigne.[15] The inventor of the essay, in fact, accompanied Camus for most of his life. As editor of *Alger républicain,* Camus played cat and mouse with French censors, inserting passages from the *Essays* without attribution, which the authorities would promptly remove, declaring them dangerous for public morale. In early 1947, when Camus went to the Alps to rest his diseased lungs, part of his daily regimen was the *Essays.*[16]

Not surprisingly, he was especially moved by Montaigne's reflections on death. "Amazing things he says of his fear in the face of death," he wrote in his notebooks after reading the essay "That to Philosophize Is to Learn to Die." Consumed by tuberculosis for half his life, Camus was fascinated by Montaigne's repeated confrontations with death. The sixteenth-century writer, under the spell of Stoicism, sought to combat the fear of death by stripping it of its strangeness and making it commonplace. "It is

uncertain where death awaits us; let us await it everywhere."
But not merely wait: for Montaigne, one must be acting
in the world the very moment death comes to take us. "I
want death to find me planting my cabbages, but careless
of death, and still more of my unfinished garden."[17]

Camus knew that Montaigne, before retiring to his
chateau to write, had served most of his life as a public
official. Not only had he been a magistrate in the Bordeaux
Parliament and city mayor during an outbreak of the bu-
bonic plague, but he had also served as go-between during an even more virulent and persistent plague: France's
Wars of Religion. Montaigne's rare ability to remain above
the fray, seemingly immune to the passions that drove
Catholics and Huguenots to murderous frenzy, made him
an invaluable interlocutor for both Henri of Navarre, the
Protestant leader, and Catherine de Medici, mother of
the Catholic king Henri III. Inevitably, these same qualities also made Montaigne a mortal enemy of the fanatics
on both sides: he was, at various times, threatened, pur-
sued, and imprisoned by both Protestants and Catholic
extremists.

Born into a Catholic family (one with possible Jewish
ancestors) that branched into the Protestant faith, Montaigne knew both worlds, but refused to declare either as
the one right world. Stunned by each side's conviction
that they alone knew the truth, shocked by the acts they
committed in support of that conviction, Montaigne refused to betray his loyalty to the claims of reason and
truth. "See the horrible impudence with which we bandy
divine reasons about, and how irreligiously we have both

rejected them and taken them again, according as fortune has changed our place in these public storms," he exclaimed. And yet, "we burn the people who say that truth must be made to endure the yoke of our need."[18]

Indeed, if only it were limited to the auto-da-fé. Yet more shocking was the cruelty displayed in the killings on both sides. The corpse of the Protestant leader Admiral de Coligny, killed with a sword thrust through the mouth, was defenestrated, beheaded, mutilated, hanged, and burned. As for obscure Protestants, their fate was no kinder. One man, Mathurin Lussault, was murdered when he answered his door, as was his son when he heard the commotion. Mathurin's wife leapt from the upstairs window to escape the mob, breaking both her legs. The crowd dragged her into the street, hacked off her hands, and skewered her on a pole. For several days, dogs were seen gnawing on her hands.[19]

Montaigne was appalled by these acts, no doubt spurring him to write an essay devoted to the subject of cruelty: "I could hardly be convinced, until I saw it, that there were souls so monstrous that they would commit murder for the mere pleasure of it; hack and cut off other men's limbs; sharpen their wits to invent unaccustomed torments and new forms of death, without enmity, without profit, and for the sole purpose of enjoying the pleasing spectacle of the pitiful gestures and movements, the lamentable groans and cries, of a man dying in anguish. For that is the uttermost point that cruelty can attain."[20]

A half-millennium later, events in Algeria revealed that little had changed. "Ja-----, smiling all the time, dangled the clasps at the end of the electrodes before my eyes. These were little shining steel clips, elongated and toothed. . . . He attached one of them to the lobe of my right ear and the other to a finger on the same side. Suddenly, I leapt in my bonds and shouted with all my might. . . . A flash of lightning exploded next to my ear and I felt my heart racing in my breast. I struggled, screaming, and stiffened myself until the straps cut into my flesh."[21] In 1958, Editions de Minuit, which began life in 1942 as a clandestine publisher committed to France's liberation, published Henri Alleg's *The Question*. An account of his arrest and torture by the "paras" (French paratroopers) engaged in the Battle of Algiers, Alleg's story awakened a nation that, until the book's publication (and the French government's failed attempt to censure it), had striven to close its eyes to the nature of the conflict. Scarcely twenty years after the Nazi occupiers and French collaborators, in their doomed effort to eradicate the Resistance, had tortured and killed hundreds of Frenchmen and women, French were now torturing Algerian men and women for the same reasons. As Alleg announced, while his "particular case is exceptional in that it has attracted public attention, it is not in any way unique."[22]

The French army's justification for the use of torture was straightforward and compelling: France was at war with a terrorist organization whose bombings and assassinations had taken the lives of hundreds of innocent Frenchmen, women, and children. Without the information extracted from arrested terrorists, or their sympathizers, yet more innocents would die. According to Marcel Bigeard, a colonel who both revolutionized French military tactics in Algeria and oversaw the use of torture, deliberately and methodically inflicting pain on the enemy was a "necessary evil." In order to underscore the gravity of France's engagement, Bigeard himself underwent water torture in order to know its effects. That he also knew it would occur just once, and that it would not stretch over hours, days, and weeks; that he knew he was a commanding officer whose authority over his "torturers" was unquestioned; and that he knew he was *staging* the experience all seem to undermine the goal of this personal experiment. While Bigeard's particular case was, like Alleg's, exceptional in the amount of attention it eventually received, it was quite unlike Alleg's because it was not representative of the practice.[23]

A few months after Alleg's book had transformed the perception of France's war in Algeria, Gallimard published *Algerian Chronicles,* Camus' collection of articles on Algeria. By then, Camus had, like Montaigne, also retired from public affairs—at least in regard to his native Algeria. After the failure of his effort to convince the warring sides to adopt a civilian truce, Camus retreated into public silence. In February 1956, shortly after the still-born civilian truce, Camus had quit his position at *L'Express,* telling friends he could no longer write or speak publicly on events in Algeria. What more could he say at this point? Silence seemed, if not the sole option, the most meaningful one. As he wrote to his friend, the Kabyle writer Mouloud Feraoun: "When language is thoughtlessly used to dispose of human lives, being silent is not a negative quality."[24]

But there was little agreement then, as there is now, on
the nature of Camus' silence. Speaking for the great majority of Parisian intellectuals, Simone de Beauvoir declared she "was revolted by [Camus'] refusal to speak."[25]
Even sympathetic critics like the Jewish Tunisian writer
Albert Memmi—whose first novel, *The Pillar of Salt,* carried
a foreword by Camus—attributed Camus' silence to a sort
of paralysis visited on "colonizers of good will" who cannot escape the impossible dilemma in which history has
placed them. "Indeed, such is Camus' situation that he
was assured of becoming the target of the suspicion of the
colonized, of the indignation of the Left of metropolitan
France, and the anger of his own people."[26]

Montaigne would have immediately recognized Camus'
plight as his own. In sixteenth-century France, extremists
among both Catholics and Protestants despised *les politiques:* moderates devoted to negotiation and compromise.
But in a nation increasingly polarized, in which each religious camp saw the other as evil incarnate, the *politiques*
were not just distrusted, but often powerless in the face
of repeated spasms of violence. Mayor of a volatile city
divided between Huguenots and Catholics, where the fanatics of the Catholic League terrorized Protestants and
politiques, Montaigne was acutely aware of his thankless
and desperate task. As he observed: "Our zeal does wonders when it is seconding our leaning towards hatred, cruelty, ambition, avarice, detraction, rebellion. Against the
grain, toward goodness, benignity, moderation, unless as
by a miracle some rare nature bears it, it will neither walk
nor fly."[27]

Yet Montaigne, though a *politique*, was not an amoralist—
to the contrary. "Among other vices," he wrote with rare
intensity, "I cruelly hate cruelty, both by nature and by
judgment, as the extreme of all vices."[28] Like Camus, he
feared those who argued that a good and great end could
justify violent and evil means. The notion of launching a
foreign war was popular among certain *politiques*, for it
would help unify the nation and put a damper on the
wars of religion. While Montaigne agreed that a foreign
conflict was a "milder evil" than civil war, he refused the
tempting proposal: "I do not believe that God would favor
so unjust an enterprise as to injure and pick a quarrel with
others for our own convenience."[29]

In a situation where truth-telling could easily be fatal,
Montaigne nevertheless insisted on candor. "I do not refrain from saying anything, however grave or burning, I
could not have said behind [others'] backs." With a nod to
the low and mean methods used by regimes, Montaigne
acknowledged the inevitability of men who "betray and
lie and massacre."[30] As for himself, he will "resign this
commission to more obedient and supple people." In his
preface to *Algerian Chronicles*, Camus seems to channel
Montaigne. In attempting to find a common ground between the two sides, he dismisses the judgment of those
who have not lived in Algeria. And as for those who have,
yet "continue to believe, heroically, that it is better for one's
brother to die than one's principles, I will limit myself to
admiring them from afar. I am not one of their race."[31]
Indeed, as his sense of separation deepened, Camus blamed
it on his insistence to *parler vrai*: "If I have always refused

to lie . . . it is because I could never accept solitude. But solitude should now also be accepted."[32]

The historian James Le Sueur underscores this state of solitude when he dismisses Camus as the "glaring exception" from the united front of French intellectuals opposed "to the violation of human rights in Algeria."[33] He was an exception, but not in the way Le Sueur seems to suggest. Camus did repeatedly condemn the French military's practice of torture and executions. Not only were these acts simply criminal, he declared, they were also politically foolhardy. In a column for *L'Express* in 1955, Camus underscored what seems obvious only in retrospect: "Each act of repression . . . [and] each act of police torture . . . has deepened the despair and violence of those subjected to them. In this way, the police have given birth to terrorists who in turn have given birth to yet more police."[34]

Three years later, in *Algerian Chronicles,* Camus agonized over the tragic harvest to this criminal and criminally myopic policy. Addressing his fellow French and French Algerians, Camus was blunt: "Reprisals against civilians and the practice of torture are crimes for which we are all responsible. That we have allowed these acts to occur is a humiliation we must henceforth confront. For now, we must at the very least reject every justification, even that of effectiveness, for such methods. From the very moment we justify them, even indirectly, neither rule nor value can exist, all claims are equally valid and war without limit or laws consecrates the triumph of nihilism."[35]

Clearly, Camus did condemn torture. But what he refused was what we might call "selective condemnation."

He was disgusted by the silence of his erstwhile friends on the French left in regard to the terrorism of the National Liberation Front (FLN), which led the struggle for Algerian independence. While the French military and intelligence services were electrocuting, water boarding, and raping FLN militants, the FLN was murdering the leaders of competing nationalist movements as well as *pied-noir* civilians. In an order issued following the execution of two FLN commanders in 1956, immediate reprisals were called for against the civilian population: "Kill any European between the ages of eighteen and fifty-four years." At the same time, female operatives for the FLN launched a series of bomb explosions at popular cafés, killing or maiming dozens of women and men. As Algeria lurched into what he called a "xenophobic delirium," Camus urged both sides to recognize their complicity. Just as "the massacre of civilians must be condemned by the Arab movement, French liberals must do the same in regard to French repression." Failing this, Camus concluded, the very notions of guilt and innocence will be drowned in the bloodshed of total war.[36]

Camus was exceptional in remaining faithful to an ethical stance that Montaigne would have recognized. "I am an average man with an exigency," he wrote in his notebook. "The values I ought to defend and illustrate today are average values. This requires a talent so spare and unadorned that I doubt I have it."[37] Among Camus' average values was the conviction that the end must never justify the means. Once this rule is violated, well-intentioned men and women will begin their race toward incompatible goals, leaving behind them the trampled remainder of humankind. In a pained journal entry, he reminded himself: "My effort now is to carry this presence of myself to myself through to the very end, to maintain it whatever aspect my life takes on—even at the price of the loneliness which I now know is so difficult to bear. Not to give way— that is the whole secret. Not to surrender, not to betray."[38]

Fidelity to his father's gut reaction upon seeing his comrades' mutilated bodies—"A man doesn't let himself do that!"—fueled Camus' lifelong opposition to capital punishment. In this regard, like Montaigne, Camus would speak truth not just to power, but to his readers as well—in some ways, a far more difficult task. As he wrote in "Reflections on the Guillotine," when "silence or tricks of language contribute to maintaining an abuse that must be reformed or a suffering that can be relieved, then there is no other solution but to speak out and show the obscenity hidden under the verbal cloak."[39]

By the late 1940s, petitioners and lawyers not just in France but across the globe were seeking Camus' support on behalf of condemned political prisoners. Camus spoke out on behalf of condemned political prisoners across the world, protesting, in the words of Eve Morisi, the " 'death-centered' state in all of its guises."[40] Camus intervened on behalf of political prisoners in Franco's Spain and Stalin's Russia, Eastern Europe, Iran, Vietnam, and Greece.

Even the United States prodded Camus, if not to intervene—since the prisoner had already been executed—at least to interrogate the nature of capital punishment. In 1959, Robert Wise's film "I Want to Live!" was released in France. The film starred Susan Hayward as Barbara Graham, a drug addict who, found guilty of the murder of a rich widow, was executed in a gas chamber. Directed in a brutally realistic manner, the film blurs the question of Graham's guilt—documents suggest she was, in fact, guilty—instead focusing on the stages of a state-sanctioned execution. Camus was deeply impressed by the film—so much so that he saw it twice and wrote a short apprecia-tion. "The merciless story this film retraces is a true story," he declared. Asserting that film, if it has any purpose at all, is "to confront us with the realities of our time," Camus concluded that Wise confronts us with a reality "we don't have the right to ignore."[41]

Never published in France, the review was nevertheless translated into English and publicized by the film's pro-ducer. An American journalist based in Los Angeles, Jack Beck, was disturbed by Camus' apparent claim that Gra-ham was, in fact, innocent. He showed, in a closely argued three-page letter to Camus, how Wise omitted a number of facts from the movie that tied Graham to the crime. Camus quickly replied to Beck, confessing that he might well have been "misinformed" about Graham's case. But what follows is no less telling: "Nevertheless, may I tell you that I am not convinced that I was wrong?" For Camus the death penalty itself remains a criminal act whether or not Graham was guilty. Indeed, he explains, "To oppose the death penalty only if the accused individual is innocent makes absolutely no sense."[42]

What gripped Camus' moral imagination was the way
in which the film recreated the reality of killing another
human being. The "quivering body dropped onto a board
to have its head cut off"—or to have its lungs filled with
poison gas, or to have its heart torn apart by bullets—
remained the fundamental datum of capital punishment.
Hence Camus' horror at any effort, by institutions or individuals representing democratic or totalitarian societies that sought to render abstract this brute fact. In a letter to his former teacher Jean Grenier, Camus recounted
how, during the postwar purge in France, he left a trial of
a Frenchman accused of treason. The accused man, Camus told Grenier, was clearly guilty. "Yet I left the trial
before the end because *I was with him* [ie., the accused]. . . .
In every guilty man, there is an element of innocence. This
is what makes any absolute condemnation revolting. We
do not think enough about pain."[43]

There is nothing abstract about pain. It is specific, it is
real and, when it is intense, it is "world-destroying."[44]
Elaine Scarry makes a fundamental point about pain:
whereas most human emotions are attached to an outside object—one is in love *with*, one is worried *by*—pain has
no such referent. "It is not *of* or *for* anything." Moreover,
Scarry argues, the very effort to objectify or analogize pain
is "itself a sign of pain's triumph, for it achieves its aver-
siveness in part by bringing about, even within a radius
of several feet, this absolute split between one's sense of
one's own reality and the reality of other persons."[45]

The dangers of abstraction preoccupied Camus. In
1947, the same year as the publication of *The Plague*, Camus

reread his *cahiers,* the school notebooks in which he had recorded his thoughts for more than a decade. The effect was sobering: "I have read over all these notebooks—beginning with the first. This was obvious to me: land-scapes gradually disappear. The modern cancer is gnawing at me too." In other words, his memory of the world—the object of his fidelity—was fading while his preoccupation with ideas grew. This same distancing struck him during a flight that same year from Paris to Algiers: "The air-plane as one of the elements of modern negation and ab-straction. There is no more nature; the deep gorge, true relief, the impassable mountain stream, everything dis-appears. There remains a *diagram*—a map. Man, in short, looks through the eyes of God. And he perceives then that God can have but an abstract view. This is not a good thing."[46]

The moral imagination, for Camus as for Simone Weil, is the work of attention. Attention to the physical world in its inflexible and indifferent attitude toward us, atten-tion to our fellow human beings in our common struggle to resist this cosmic indifference. Shortly after France's liberation, Camus wrote a series of articles for *Combat* ti-tled "Neither Victims nor Executioners." The articles were, in part, inspired by conversations Camus had in Paris with Arthur Koestler, whose damning analysis of totalitarian-ism in *Darkness At Noon* and *The Yogi and the Commissar* had won him fame on both sides of the Atlantic. But Ca-mus' essays also reflect Weil's portrayal of the ways in which force, be it war or factories or governments, trans-forms human beings into things. "Neither Victims nor

Executioners" is both an echo and reply to Weil's claim that those who wield power are no less its victims than those who are subjected to it. Finally the articles flow from Camus' lifelong attachment to the particular and concrete, and his enduring suspicion of the general and abstract. As he declared in the opening article, "The Century of Fear," we have lost the habit of speaking "the language of humanity" founded on the everyday realities of our lives when we "confront the beauty of the world and people's faces." In each instance of these crimes, Camus wrote, "it was impossible to persuade the people who were doing these things not to do them, because they were sure of themselves and because there is no way of persuading an abstraction."[47]

In his effort to "save bodies" carried atop the floodwaters of history, Camus diagnoses one of "the faults of our century": people attached to the language of ideology or bureaucracy, he states, "lack imagination when it comes to other people's deaths. . . . Just as we now love one another by telephone and work not on matter but on machines, we kill and are killed by proxy. What is gained in cleanliness is lost in understanding."[48] In order to salvage our understanding, moral and experiential, Camus insists we push aside the usual clichés we use and instead describe as faithfully as possible what it means to kill another man in a manner so methodical and deliberate. Rather than telling the doomed prisoner that he will atone for or repay society for his act, we should inform him that he "will be imprisoned for months or years, torn between an impossible despair and a constantly renewed terror." And then, one day, he shall be carried, his hands tied behind his back and feet "dragging behind in the corridor" to the scaffold. An executioner will "finally seize you by the seat of your pants and throw you horizontally on a board while another will steady your head in the lunette and a third will let fall from a height of seven feet a hundred-and-twenty-pound blade that will slice off your head like a razor."[49]

Thus the power of his essay "Reflections on the Guillotine," published in 1957 with an accompanying piece by Koestler. At the outset, Camus warns us he will not speak politely about the nature of capital punishment. Instead, "it is my intention to talk about it crudely"—though not for the sake of sensationalism or sadism. We must never tolerate a certain kind of silence, Camus announces: the kind of silence born from moral lassitude or social convention. "When silence or verbal trickery helps to maintain an abuse that needs to be ended or suffering that needs to be soothed, there is no choice but to speak out and show the obscenity disguised by a cloak of words."[50]

Camus does not end his recital here, but instead turns to the physiological reaction of the body when its head is severed—we learn, for instance, that Charlotte Corday's "severed head blushed from the executioner's slap"—as well as the psychological reaction of those—such as other prisoners—who watch repeated executions. As for those of us reading these accounts, Camus is trenchant: "The man who enjoys his coffee while reading that justice has been done would spit it out at the least detail."[51] A far better reaction, of course, than savoring one's coffee while

the blade thumped, but the consequences—a human being reduced to a headless lump of flesh and a "society reduced to a state of primitive terrors where nothing can be
judged"—remain the same.[52]

In language made taut by suppressed outrage, Camus
details what happens to a human being subjected to the
legal, social, and technical mechanisms that form the
machinery of state-sanctioned killing. He underscores
the hypocrisy of official claims that the death penalty has
an exemplary or preventative function: if this were the
case, he notes, the state would not hide the apparatus or
final act from the public's view. "Today there is no spectacle, but only a penalty we know only by hearsay along with
the occasional announcement of an execution gussied up
in gentle phrases."[53] Would it not be more consistent, he
asks, to instead distribute to all citizens a detailed report
of what happens to a living body once its head is removed?
Or, even more effective, "show us the severed head" while
we ready ourselves for a new day.[54]

A danger with charging others with a lack of moral imagination is that one will conclude that, if guilty, they also
lack the right of living among the rest of us. For a brief
period, Camus demanded on France's behalf both the
right to judge and execute the guilty. In the summer and
fall of 1944, as liberated France struggled with its immediate past and chaotic present, he wrote an editorial in
the clandestine journal *Les Lettres françaises,* defending

Charles de Gaulle's decision to execute Pierre Pucheu, a former minister of interior under Vichy, who had ordered the execution of resistance fighters. "Too many men have died who we loved and respected," he declared, "too many splendors betrayed, too many values humiliated . . . even for those of us in the midst of this battle who would otherwise be tempted to pardon him."[55]

Though heinous, Pucheu's treason was not his greatest crime. Instead, Camus declared, it was his "lack of imagination"—his inability to attend to the world and the consequences of his actions. As the Vichy bureaucrat who oversaw the nation's police forces, Pucheu acted as if nothing had changed since France's defeat and occupation. A creature of the "abstract and administrative system he had always known," Pucheu, in the comfort of his office, signed laws condemning men to death. These papers, signed and stamped, would be "transformed into dawns of terror for innocent Frenchmen led to their deaths."[56]

Pucheu's particular crime forced Camus to measure fully his own words: "it is in the full light of our imagination that we are learning to accept without flinching . . . that a man's life can be removed from this world."[57] In his editorials immediately following France's liberation, Camus focused on this same "banal" flaw. At the end of August, reacting to the torture and murder of thirty-four Frenchmen by members of Vichy's murderous *milice,* he exclaimed: "Who would dare speak here of forgiveness?" Once again, his outrage focuses on the torturer's lack of imagination. After describing the state of the corpses, Camus forces us to imagine what led up to their deaths: "Two men face to face, one of whom prepares to tear off the fingernails of the other who watches him do it."[58] Was there a place in postwar France for men who committed such crimes? No, replied Camus. As he had declared in an earlier editorial: "No one any longer has the *right* to lack imagination. . . . The time for abstractions is over."[59]

Until, that is, the revolutionary purge collapsed into a series of increasingly inconsistent trials, accompanied by summary acts of revenge parading as justice. As Camus' disgust deepened, Robert Brasillach's trial took place. A novelist and essayist who was an ardent collaborationist, Brasillach was found guilty of treason and sentenced to death in early 1945. The writer Marcel Aymé, who launched a petition to General de Gaulle asking that he commute Brasillach's sentence to life imprisonment, certainly did not lack imagination: he asked Camus for his signature.

François Mauriac, whose resistance and literary credentials were equal to those of Camus, had already signed the petition. Devoutly Catholic, Mauriac had previously collided with Camus on the question of the purge. The older man insisted on the need for mercy and national reconciliation, while the young editor of *Combat* replied that national healing required a foundation built on implacable justice. When the trials had turned into sham events, however, Camus confessed in an editorial: "We now see that M. Mauriac was right: we are going to need charity."[60] Yet when Mauriac refused to let him off the hook—he disdainfully thanked "our young master" for having spoken from the "heights of the works he has yet to write"—Camus retorted that Mauriac's brand of mercy was irrelevant for the generation that he, Camus, represented. Christianity meant nothing for "those in this tormented world who believe that Christ may have died to save others, but that he did not die to save us." As a result, "we will forever refuse a divine charity which frustrates the justice of men."[61]

Yet Camus signed Brasillach's petition. Reinvesting with all of its complexity his earlier claim that "no one any longer has the *right* to lack imagination," Camus spent the sleepless night before signing by dwelling on the reality of the fate that awaited Brasillach. As he explained in his accompanying letter to Aymé: "I have always held the death sentence in horror and judged that, at least as an individual, I couldn't participate in it, even by abstention. That's all. And this is a scruple that I suppose would make Brasillach's friends laugh."[62]

This same scruple drove Camus, especially after his silence on the civil war, to intercede on behalf of Algerians condemned to death by the French courts. Until the recent publication of several dozen letters he exchanged with lawyers and politicians, Camus' remarkable role in these cases was mostly unknown. Among his most persistent correspondents was his friend Yves Dechezelles: fellow students at the University of Algiers, both men joined

Combat during the war. Having established a law practice in Algiers, Dechezelles belonged to the besieged minority of liberal *pieds-noirs* who, like Camus, fought on behalf of the Arab and Berber communities. Not surprisingly, Dechezelles was at Camus' side in January 1956, when he gave his Algiers speech calling for a civilian truce. In their letters, the friends address one another in the familiar "tu"—a rarity for Camus, who addressed even his close friend René Char in the formal "vous."

In late July 1957, a French court's decision to condemn three Algerian militants to death threatened to derail faltering negotiations between France and the FLN. More important, Dechezelles, who represented the men, made clear that the sentences were politically motivated. One of the men, Badeche Ben Hamdi, seems to have been innocent of the charge of murder, while no deaths occurred in the two other cases. These cases, Dechezelles frantically explained to Camus, "are based on absolutely no conception of justice." Telling his old friend that he was "obsessed" by the executions and "frightened" over their consequences, Dechezelles was also scandalized that France's political leaders, so as not to be "troubled by [*pied-noir*] extremists," will allow "a contingent of heads to fall." Whether by writing a newspaper or making a public speech, or intervening with the president or other political leader, Dechezelles pleaded with Camus to act: "My God, you've got to shout."[63]

Two days after Dechezelles' plea, there followed a second one from his colleague Gisèle Halimi, a Tunisian

Jewish lawyer who was then launching a career as a civil rights lawyer that would span half a century. In 1956, when Camus met Halimi for the first time, he told her: "If I can help you with certain cases, call me."[64] Halimi did not need to be asked twice: writing with tremendous urgency, she summarized the three cases and—with a lawyerly twist—cited Camus' own "Reflections on the Guillotine" as an argument for his intervention. She had no need to add that the executions would take place at Barberousse prison—the same prison where Camus' father witnessed the execution that marked not just his life, but also his son's. As the bureaucracy of death so meticulously described by Camus hummed louder, Halimi concluded: "You must help us."[65]

Which is what Camus did—though not publicly and perhaps not always consistently with his own writings. Unwilling to break his silence on Algeria, Camus instead carefully reviewed the cases—his private papers contain long and detailed descriptions he wrote for each case—and wrote to President René Coty. Largely a ceremonial position in France's Fourth Republic, the president nevertheless had the power to pardon prisoners. In his letter, Camus made explicit the basis of his request: none of the condemned men were guilty of "either the blind attacks or repugnant terrorism that strikes the civilian population, whether French or Muslim." Camus reminds Coty that he is a French Algerian whose family still lives there, and that the "current drama echoes daily within me." His public reserve, he concludes, is perhaps justification enough for him to ask Coty to consider pardoning these men, if only to "preserve what little remains of Algeria's future."[66]

Coty acknowledged his receipt of Camus' letter, but did not respond directly to Camus' request. Subsequent events, though, were expressive enough. As Camus tersely noted in a letter to Prime Minister Guy Mollet, almost all of the prisoners whose lives he tried to save had been executed.[67] (This was not always the case. A letter he sent to Charles de Gaulle in 1959 on behalf of three condemned men appears to have influenced the general, who subsequently commuted their sentences.) In his letters to Coty and Mollet, as with de Gaulle after he came to power in 1958, Camus always recalled the immense power clothing these men through their elected positions. And behind these reminders hovers Camus' insistence on the reality behind cold and bureaucratic phrases. He never wanted his interlocutors to elide or hide from the sheer *finality* of the capital punishment. This had already been a preoccupation when he was still a reporter for *Alger républicain*. In an editorial seeking the intervention of Algeria's most powerful official, the governor general, in the case of Michel Hodent, who had been imprisoned on false charges, Camus spoke as one man to another: while "we glimpse you in processions, laws and speeches," he asked, "where do we find the man in all of that?" And yet, behind the pomp and scenery, Camus observes, there is a *human being:* the governor general is just one man among others. It is to this man of flesh and blood, who will one day know the terror of death, that Camus appeals on behalf of a fellow man. To save the life of an individual "in a world where the humanity of so many others is lost to absurdity and misery . . . amounts to saving oneself."[68]

While Camus reminded Mollet in one of his letters that he was opposed to capital punishment as a "general principle"—this, after all, is the fruit of "Reflections on the Guillotine"—fierce emotional and time pressures tested this principle. At times, he clearly makes a tactical decision: in a letter to Mollet, he begins by declaring "he will leave aside the human element [to capital punishment] of which you are aware."[69] Instead, Camus reviews the practical and political reasons for commuting the death sentences, all of which share the same goal: preserving an Algeria where French and Arabs would coexist peacefully.

It may also be for tactical reasons that, at times, Camus seems willing to ignore the human element altogether, as when he distinguishes between those acts that did not take civilian lives and "blind acts of terrorism." Indeed, in her memoir, Halimi recounts that after another request to Camus for assistance, he replied: "I despise the murderers of women and children." On that day, she writes, Camus "refused to help me."[70]

But the precise nature of Camus' refusal remains obscure. In fact, the archival documents suggest that the only time Camus turned down such a request was in February 1958. The writer Bernard Clavel wrote to him, asking if he would accept leadership of a movement to abolish the death penalty. But Camus' secretary, Suzanne Agnely, replied that he was too ill to reply, much less assume such a

task. All the more so as his illness, in the wake of receiv-
ing the Nobel Prize a few weeks earlier, seemed as much
emotional as physical: subject to fits of asphyxiation, Camus avoided walking in public, terrified that he would be
recognized by strangers.[71]

At the heart of Homer's *Odyssey* is the reuniting of a father and son who never knew one another. The epic begins with the son, Telemachus, leaving Ithaka in search
of news of the father who, twenty years later, he believes
is dead. Of course, it is only upon his return that he finds
Odysseus alive, well, and preparing to reclaim his rule. But
what if Telemachus, years into his pursuit of his father,
instead stumbled across a burial site on a far-flung Aegean
isle on which his father's name and age are inscribed. With
the force of a god's blow, Telemachus reels under the realization he has lived longer than did the father at whose
tomb he is standing.

   This, at least, is the variation on Homer's story we find
in *The First Man*. When Jacques Cormery visits the cemetery in Saint-Brieuc and discovers his father's gravestone,
he realizes he is now older than his father had been when
he died, a father "who had died unknown on this earth
where he had fleetingly passed, like a stranger."[72] Like
Telemachus, Cormery is told he is a "spitting image" of the
father he never knew.[73] And, like Telemachus as he sets out
to find news, Cormery tells himself: "It was not too late; he
could still search, he could learn who this man had been

who now seemed closer to him than any other being on this earth. He could . . ."

And he did, in part, by remaining faithful to the one memory of his father passed down to him.

5

REVOLT

On December 17, 2010, history descended on the Tunisian town of Sidi Bouzid. At midday, a fruit vendor by the name of Mohamed Bouazizi walked to offices of the regional government. Standing in the street outside the entrance, he doused himself with a can of gasoline and struck a match to his clothing. By the time the flames were stamped out, Bouazizi's body had been almost entirely scorched. Though he lived for another eighteen days, the young man never woke from his coma. By the time he was buried on January 4, 2011, the first tremors of Arab Spring were rippling from Sidi Bouzid across North Africa and the Middle East.

Earlier that day, the local officials, under the pretext that Bouazizi did not have a vendor's license, overturned his cart and confiscated his scales. For good measure, they also slapped and spat on him. The sole breadwinner for a family of eight, Bouazizi was too poor to pay the usual bribe required in such situations. It was only after his complaints to the police went unheeded that Bouazizi walked to a nearby gas station, bought enough gasoline to soak his clothing, and returned to the governor's building. Shouting "How do you expect me to make a living?" Mohamed Bouazizi already knew the answer. The match he lit served not just as an exclamation mark, but also as the mark of rebellion. In effect, Bouazizi asked: "How can you expect me to accept the life you impose on me?"

To the only philosophical question worth asking—whether suicide must be our response to an absurd world—Camus' reply was clear: it cannot and must not be. If, as he wrote in *The Myth of Sisyphus,* "revolt gives life its value," suicide instead accepts—embraces, even—a life and world devoid of meaning and importance. It is essential, he affirmed, "to die unreconciled and not of one's own free will. Suicide is a repudiation. The absurd man can only drain everything to the bitter end. . . . The absurd is his extreme tension, which he maintains constantly by solitary effort, for he knows that in that consciousness and in that day-to-day revolt he gives proof of his only truth, which is defiance."[1]

By all accounts a thoughtful and responsible man, Mohamed Bouazizi had most probably not read Camus. But if he had, would he have disputed the claim that suicide is tantamount to acceptance of the way things are—a gesture of despair? In his fictionalized account of Bouazizi's act, the French novelist Tahar Ben Jelloun tries to recreate the final images flickering across the young man's mind: "the official who spat on him, the other who insulted him ... his mother and sisters waiting in line for water, policemen harassing him, insults and blows, insults and blows."[2] In a word, the repeated outrages to his dignity. We cannot know, of course, if this was so. What we do know, however, is that millions of young men and women instead interpreted his last gesture as an act of defiance and rebellion. "Yesterday it was Camus ... today it is Bouazizi," affirmed a young Tunisian intellectual: "He is perhaps no longer part of our world, but he is not silent. ... His cry is primal: he demands the right to dignity, to work. He demands the right to enjoy the rights all humans should enjoy."[3]

Camus was writing against the deadly sophistries of communism and its penchant for rationalizing mass murder and political repression. But he would also have written in these terms against the political crimes in North Africa, equally liable to forms of logical justification that most often are packaged as "political realism." Apologists for the autocratic states along the southern shore of the Mediterranean had long emphasized the necessity of order over democracy, the status quo over the uncertainties of change. We were asked to overlook the corruption and brutality of these states; when we had no choice but to gaze at it, we tended to excuse it in the same paternalistic terms that Egyptian leaders used even as they were being pushed out the door: the people are not ready for democracy.

As Camus wrote of rebellions past and present, the youth of North Africa are reacting to "the spectacle of irrationality, confronted with an unjust and incomprehensible condition." For young Egyptians under an octogenarian *rais* propped by a murderous police force and billions in American military aid, for young Tunisians under a kleptocratic ruler whose family considered the nation a warehouse to pillage, and for young Libyans under a murderous lunatic whose rule rivaled Caligula's over Rome, the moment finally arrived, as Camus writes, that "the outrage be brought to an end."[4]

With *The Rebel,* Camus seemingly shifts from the earlier focus of *The Myth of Sisyphus:* suicide's place in the philosophical docket is now taken by homicide. Declaring that he and his contemporaries live in the "era of premeditation and the perfect crime," Camus insists we "shall know nothing until we know whether we have the right to kill our fellow men, or the right to let them be killed."[5]

Whereas Camus does not connect the earlier essay with the realities of its time—at least if he expected it to be published under the watchful eyes of German censors—*The Rebel* directly confronts the ideologies that made possible that same era. One might think, he observes, that a period which "in the space of fifty years, uproots, enslaves, or kills seventy million human beings should be condemned out of hand." But it is not so easy, he warns: we must also try to understand this era's "culpability."[6] We incur our historical as well as metaphysical guilt, Camus discovers, when we allow the act of rebellion to grow into—or, rather, be reduced to—revolution.

In the weeks and months that followed France's liberation and Germany and Japan's defeat, as the abyss deepened between the United States and Soviet Russia, Camus had already begun to explore the distinction between the rebel and revolutionary. In his 1946 series of editorials titled "Neither Victims Nor Executioners," Camus declared that terror transfixed the world. Why? Because "persuasion is no longer possible, because man has been delivered entirely into the hands of history . . . because we live in a world of abstraction, a world of bureaucracy and machinery, of absolute ideas and of messianism without subtlety. We gasp for air among people who believe they are absolutely right, whether it be in their machines or their ideas."[7]

Communist Russia, of course, did not have a monopoly on machines and machinery, abstractions and bureaucracies. Camus was intensely preoccupied by these same tendencies in American culture and politics. His voice, along with that of François Mauriac, was the only one in the French press to recoil at the news of Hiroshima. In an editorial published in the short space between the bombings of Hiroshima and Nagasaki, Camus announced that the "civilization of the machine has just achieved its ultimate degree of savagery." Rather than celebrating this event, which smacked of "indecency," Camus instead urged a moment's reflection. But he was not optimistic on reflection's results: "Even before now it was not easy to breathe in this tormented world. Now we find ourselves confronted with a new source of anguish, which has every likelihood of proving fatal. Mankind has probably been given its last chance, and the papers have seized on this as a pretext for a special edition: 'Extra! Extra! Read all about it!'"[8]

While the banalization of violence was worrisome, even more disquieting were the efforts made to legitimate it. For this reason, Camus was scandalized by the position taken by friends on the French Left who believed that communism was at least building a better—or, in the era's phrase—"a singing tomorrow." The unlikely chorus master for this particular refrain was Maurice Merleau-Ponty, whose book *Humanism and Terror* was serialized shortly before Camus began writing "Neither Victims nor Executioners." A phenomenologist whose work deeply influenced Jean-Paul Sartre, Merleau-Ponty refused to blink at the brutal reality of the Soviet Union. It was clear, he noted, that the USSR was a far cry from the "the proletarian light of History Marx once described." Nevertheless, Merleau-Ponty continued, not only did the existence of Soviet labor camps fail to discredit Marxism, but they also failed to condemn the Soviet experiment. Only history, in its unfolding, will "give us the final word as to the legitimacy of a particular instance of violence." No less important, and even more disturbingly, Merleau-Ponty then observed that violence pulsed through the veins of all societies. But there are different blood types: the communist variety was vastly preferable to the capitalist one. The question, Merleau-Ponty concluded, was "where a form of violence fits in the meaning of history, and whether it carries with it the promise of the negation of future violence."[9]

In short, while it contained toxins, the blood of communism would eventually pulse through a revitalized body politic, while the blood of capitalism was itself a toxin that condemned the body to death—or, more accurately, to meaningless. Like many others on the French Left—or, for that matter, anywhere else on the ideological spectrum—Merleau-Ponty could not accept the prospect that history had no prospect, that it was empty of meaning and deprived of a particular end. Marxism alone invests history with both a meaning and an end. For this reason, it is not just a philosophy of history, but it is *"the* philosophy of history and to denounce it is to dig the grave of Reason in history. After that there can be no more dreams or adventures."[10]

Merleau-Ponty never directly responded to Camus' series of articles. To do so, perhaps, would have been redundant. Shortly after Merleau-Ponty published a section of his own book in *Les Temps modernes,* the influential journal edited by Sartre and Beauvoir, Camus bumped into him during a party at a mutual friend's apartment. An argument over the article erupted between the two; Sartre rushed to the defense of Merleau-Ponty, who seemed taken aback by Camus' furious attack. The confrontation ended only when Camus, in a white anger, quit the apartment. Sartre rushed out after him and, without success, tried to persuade Camus to return to the party. Though Camus' friendship with Sartre survived the firefight, the battle lines between the *pied-noir* and his Parisian friends were being drawn.

Indeed, the line was more deeply etched by Emmanuel d'Astier de la Vigerie. An aristocrat whose intellectual career had begun in the 1920s on the far right and steadily moved leftward, particularly after his engagement in the Spanish Civil War and French Resistance, when he entered the orbit of the French Communist Party, d'Astier is one of the most striking figures in *The Sorrow and the Pity*, Marcel Ophuls' celebrated documentary on Vichy France. With a mane of white hair framing a high forehead and a pipe ensconced in his gracefully gesticulating hand, d'Astier famously described resistance fighters as natural misfits: men and women who, unable to find a place in peacetime society, discovered themselves only during the war and occupation.

And yet, as the postwar editor of the newspaper *Libération*, subsidized by the French Communist Party, d'Astier seemed determined to fit into their particular view of the world. Upon the publication of "Neither Victims nor Executioners," d'Astier gave Camus an ear-boxing in the guise of a review. By condemning all forms of violence out of hand, wrote d'Astier, Camus denied the revolutionary raison d'être of the Resistance. In a metaphor that must have deeply cut Camus, d'Astier reasoned that his fellow resistance fighter might just as well support a movement for the eradication of tuberculosis without providing it with the means of doing so. Instead, for d'Astier, Camus had become little more than an apologist for liberalism and the status quo of western societies. At times only violence—as the title of his review declared—could pry the victim from the grasp of the executioner.[11]

As Camus made clear in his reply, d'Astier's brief on behalf of political violence begged the question at hand. Camus knew that violence is unavoidable: "the years under the Occupation taught me this." What he had always refused, though, was to mistake its ineluctability for legitimization. "Violence is at one and the same time unavoidable and unjustifiable." As a result, our duty is to quarantine violence, to make its use exceptional, and to recall, as vividly and clearly as possible, what it does to both those who use it and those against whom it is used. "I have a horror of easy violence," Camus told d'Astier, "I have a horror of those whose words go beyond their actions. It is for this reason that I stand apart from those great minds and [those] whose appeals to murder I will despise until they themselves use the executioner's gun."[12]

Merleau-Ponty, who enjoyed quoting a line from Antoine de Saint-Exupéry—"Man is a network of relationships, and these alone matter to him"—would perhaps have explained his confrontation in terms of Camus' uneasy ties to the world of French intellectuals.[13] Yet, for this working class *pied-noir,* whose experiences and expectations differed so dramatically from his circle of Parisian friends, there was something else, something deeper that matters to human beings—namely, the quest for a meaning to the world and our lives. Or, more precisely, there is the elusive, but insistent need for something or someone that stands outside our lives and world, and thus justifies both it and us.

Absurdity, or the world's silence in the face of our demand, lies at the end of this pursuit. But while this end is foreordained, our response is not. Our deepest impulse, once we realize the silence will never end, is to refuse this state of affairs. To shout "No" to the world as it is, to shout "Yes" to the world as it should be. Rebellion, Camus declares, is "born of the spectacle of irrationality, confronted with an unjust and incomprehensible condition. But its blind impulse is to demand order in the midst of chaos, and unity in the very heart of the ephemeral. It protests, it demands, it insists that the outrage be brought to an end, and that what has up to now been built upon shifting sands should henceforth be founded on rock."[14]

The rub was that too many men and women, unable to live with this standing outrage to their intelligence, had taken mirages for reality. Where meaning was not to be discovered, it was simply imposed on the chaos of history. Although meaning is not the same as the aim of action, as Hannah Arendt warned, but crystallizes in the human mind only after the acts are accomplished, modern ideologies confounded the two concepts.[15] This was particularly the case with communism, which affirmed that history's end would arrive with the victory of the working class and birth of the classless society. Inevitably, the making of this history entails the breaking of countless men and women. But, as Camus asked grimly, what does it matter? "In this New Jerusalem, echoing with the roar of miraculous machinery, who will still remember the cry of the victim?"[16]

A sterling and paradoxical example was Merleau-Ponty's own willingness to abide the crimes of communism for the sake of rescuing meaning. Like Immanuel Kant, who dreaded that history, without the belief that progress existed, was "a meaningless course of human affairs" or a tableau of "melancholy haphazardness," Merleau-Ponty was mortified by the same prospect. To prevent history from collapsing into farce, Merleau-Ponty wagered that reason, codified by Marxism, guaranteed history's meaning—or, which amounted to the same thing, realized its ends. For Camus, both communists and their fellow travelers were thus eager to bury their solitude "in the bosom of the armed masses, covering the emptiness of their negations with stubborn scholasticism, still directed toward the future, which it has made its only god, but separated from it by a multitude of nations that must be overthrown and continents that must be dominated."[17]

As editor of *Combat,* Camus had insisted on the necessity of moving from the act of resistance against the Germans to the act of revolution against an unjust social and economic order. As he reminded his readers in the weeks that followed France's liberation, revolution is not rebellion. "What sustained the Resistance for four years was rebellion. In other words, total, uncompromising, initially almost blind refusal to accept an order that sought to put men on their knees. Rebellion begins with the heart. But there comes a time when it moves on to the mind, when feeling turns into idea, when spontaneous enthusiasm culminates in concerted action. That is the moment of revolution."[18]

It was just a few months before, on March 15, 1944, that the "Program of the CNL" began to circulate in Nazi-occupied France. The document was the work of the National Council of Liberation, a grouping of representatives from the nation's resistance movements and political parties, whose immediate task was to coordinate the liberation of France with the Allies and General de Gaulle's Free French. The Charter, as the program came to be called, was a heroic effort to link France's imminent liberation to a series of events first begun with the taking of the Bastille. As another underground paper, *Les Cahiers politiques,* declared, the postwar resistance would "take up the broken thread of 1789." This meant nothing less than "a true democracy, freed from the reign of money, a power derived from the people but strong and stable, the equitable disposition, by the nation, of our common riches, a dignified life for free workers, the sharing of economic responsibilities by all and no longer only by a few."[19]

The Charter both echoed and codified this idealism. In its preamble, the authors affirmed that the struggle against the Nazis would continue against the oppressive social and political forces that had been entrenched in France before the war. Only then could the nation reclaim its "moral and social balance and again reveal its greatness and unity to the world." In order to reach this end, the Charter proposed a host of economic, political and social laws. Several demands, such as "respect for the human person" and "absolute equality for all citizens before the law," referred most immediately to the bloody reality of the occupation. The Charter also called for the "setting up of a true economic and social democracy," the "return to the nation of the great monopolies," the "rational organization of the economy assuring that particular interests obey the general interest," and the "participation of employees in the management of their companies." Moreover, the Charter demanded the creation of full social security, including health insurance and retirement pensions, along with the establishment of fair wages.[20]

The Charter dovetailed with many of the economic and political demands that Camus fired off in his *Combat* editorials. In his recent biography, Michel Onfray insists that Camus cannot be fully understood without first acknowledging his embrace of France's tradition of radical syndicalism, particularly in the work of the nineteenth-century theorist Jean-Pierre Proudhon, who argued that only workers' cooperatives could provide the basis for an equitable and just society. To be sure, Camus glimpsed a better future in a world organized along such lines. "I am not really a socialist," he declared; instead, "my sympathies are with the radical forms of syndicalism."[21] Time and again, Camus denounced the role of "Argent" (money): the Resistance, he warned, "will have accomplished only an infinitesimal part of our task if the French Republic of tomorrow were to find itself, like the Third Republic, under the strict control of Money." Camus instead called for a "true people's democracy," insisting that "any polity that cuts itself off from the working class is pointless and that the France of tomorrow will be what the working class becomes."[22]

Yet as Onfray himself admits, Camus' references to Proudhon are rare, as are his references to nineteenth-century revolutionary syndicalism.[23] Camus was a peculiar sort of revolutionary, less a Proudhonian, or a Marxist, than a moralist. When one of d'Astier's colleagues had questioned his familiarity with Marx's writings, in particular his analysis of freedom, Camus' response was visceral, proud, and bound to irritate his critics even further: "It is true. It was misery that taught me about freedom. But most of you have no idea what the word means."[24] Having lived his life among those who were the ostensible beneficiaries of communism, Camus had no patience with theory and its practitioners. As with Pucheu and his German friend, so too with Cold War ideologues on the Right and Left: they "lack imagination when it comes to other people's deaths."

Camus was disturbed by the sense of mission that informed American foreign policy. On the one hand, Camus deeply respected Roosevelt, seeing him as a fellow *résistant* engaged in a war against both personal illness and murderous ideologies: "His laughter was . . . of a hard won serenity, the kind that one finds after an infirmity has been overcome" and his "apparent happiness was not that of comfort, nor that of a mind too limited to perceive mankind's distress."[25] But Camus also worried about the strain of American righteousness, and was as loath to see France model itself after America as after Russia.[26] When he briefly visited New York in 1946, he was struck by American spontaneity and generosity. At the end of his lecture at Columbia University, aptly titled "The Human Crisis," it was announced that the money from the ticket sales, earmarked for French children, had been stolen. In response, the audience did not just match the original amount, but increased it. At the same time, "this desert of iron and cement" numbed Camus, as did the striking disparity in wealth.[27] In his notebook, Camus wrote: "Night on the Bowery. Poverty—and a European wants to say,: 'Finally, reality.' The utterly derelict . . . And, several steps away, the most splendid bridal shops one can imagine."[28]

More elusively, Camus was disturbed by the willed innocence of Americans. Meeting a group of students at Vassar—"What they do here for young people is worth remembering"—Camus observed that they suffered from a kind of misplaced nostalgia. "In this country where everything is done to prove that life isn't tragic, they feel something is missing."[29] That Camus had a relapse of tuberculosis during his short visit certainly influenced his bleak observations, but something deeper was also at work. Staring out of a train window as he traveled to Montreal, he was impressed, and disturbed, by "this big country, calm and slow. One feels that it has been completely unaware of the war. In the course of a few years Europe, which was several centuries ahead in knowledge, moved several centuries ahead in moral consciousness."[30]

Notebook entries lend themselves, of course, to caricature as often as concision. Camus' brief for Europe's superior "knowledge" is as puzzling as it is punchy, while Europe's ostensibly deeper moral awareness, thanks to the war and Holocaust, did little to prevent its subsequent wars of decolonization abroad and genocides at home. Still, to rebuke Camus for remarks about a nation he scarcely knew makes no more sense than to dismiss Tacitus for his equally sweeping remarks on the Germanic tribes he had never set eyes on. Neither writer was a historian; instead, they were moralists who took their respective barbarians as foils to better understand, or criticize, their own civilizations.

It may well be that this same innocence made Americans largely immune to the lure of communism. (But also preoccupied: Camus was delayed for several hours at New York customs for what most probably were his political views, while J. Edgar Hoover read with great care the articles on Camus and his fellow "existentialists" that Hannah Arendt was sending to the *Nation* magazine from Europe.[31]) Tellingly, it is in the same journal he kept in New York that Camus continued to reflect on the ideological ills besetting Europe, in particular communism. "The idea of messianism at the base of all fanaticism," he wrote: "Messianism against man."[32] Long before it became a commonplace, Camus revealed the millenarian element to what he called this "kingdom of ends."[33] He seized on the reasons for its attraction, as he did on its danger. Communism, he argued, was based on the conviction that history flowed toward a secularized day of judgment, one that climaxed with the earthly salvation of the working class. "What in fact does the sacrifice of individual men matter as long as it contributes to the salvation of all mankind. . . . Progress will cease to inflict torture after the industrial apocalypse when the day of reconciliation comes." As for the proletariat, "through its suffering and struggles, it is Christ in human form redeeming the collective sin of alienation."[34]

There are fewer communists now waiting for the end of days than there are Christians awaiting theirs. This was not the case, though, in a postwar Europe as yet under the thrall of Soviet communism. Camus decided to become, in Tony Judt's phrase, the "spokesman for the obvious."[35] The rub, of course, is that back then few people on the Left thought it obvious. The forcefulness of Camus' attack on an ideology that exercised enormous influence over French politics as well as the politics of the Left Bank may well have resulted from his own engagement with communism as a student in Algiers. His uneasiness over this chapter from his past, perhaps, drove him to make the chapters yet to be written as honest and decisive as possible.

But more simply, as Judt suggests, Camus was driven by his persistent "concern for justice."[36] It was not that he sought a world where people do not kill one another—no sane person could ever hold this as a goal—but instead "a world in which murder is not legitimized." His "modest" goal, as a result, was to "save bodies"—indeed, bodies enough "to keep open the possibility of a future."[37] If this goal was ever to be realized, Camus believed, he had to make clear, to himself and the world, the world of difference between rebellion and revolution.

"Nemesis always had a friend with her, Aidos. One day their names would be translated as Vengeance and Shame, but at the time we're talking of, when they had only just emerged from the black cloud, their natures were far more complex and variegated. What did they have in common? The notion of offense. Aidos held people back from offending. Nemesis represented the ineluctable consequences of offending. They were united in a vision of life as something that gets wounded and then, as it writhes, wounds in its turn."[38]

Roberto Calasso, in his set of variations on Greek myths, reminds us that Greek artists, from the epics through tragedy, continuously reflected on the concept of limit, recasting but never revising its fundamental character. Thus, Homer recounts how the suitors at Ithaka, having spurned Aidos by violating the rules of *xenia,* were in turned slaughtered by Nemesis in the form of Odysseus. Centuries later, Aeschylus's Prometheus, by giving man the gift of fire, oversteps the limits imposed by Zeus, who in turn bolts the outlaw fast to a rock for all eternity.

Nemesis did not exit with the entry of reason in fifth-century Greece; it simply changed appearances. From a divinity, it became a principle. This is particularly the case with the historians, for whom it governed the flux of events. In Herodotus' account of the Persian Wars, an adviser to Xerxes advises against the invasion of Greece:

"Do you see how it is the living things that exceed others in size that the god strikes with lightning and will not let them show their grandeur, while the little ones do not itch the god to action?"[39] Of course, Xerxes did not see how it was, marched west to wound the Greeks, and was wounded in turn.

In *The Rebel*, Camus briefly refers to Xerxes' spectacular "wounding" of the Greeks—namely, his invasion of the peninsula and burning of Athens—followed by the fatal wound he receives in return: the destruction of his fleet and pell-mell retreat to Persia. The occasion recounted by Camus is Xerxes's whipping of the Bosphorus when a storm delayed his invasion of Greece. "The acme of excess to the Greek mind was to beat the sea with rods—an act of insanity worthy only of barbarians."[40] But rather than continue the story in *The Rebel*, moving from the Persian Wars to the Peloponnesian War, Camus instead picks it up in his novel *The Plague*, part of the same "Promethean" cycle as his essay.

Camus read Herodotus' successor, Thucydides, with particular care when he was living in Chambon-sur-Lignon in late 1942. He had gone to this mountain village to rest his battered lungs, but found the time and distance to reflect on the limits of the absurd, if only as a basis for action in a world besieged by totalitarian forces. He began to sketch out the work that would become his novel of a plague-besieged city and how its denizens respond, published in 1947. A character in one of the early drafts, a classics teacher named Stephan, realizes "that he had not understood Thucydides until he himself experienced the plague."[41] The same was true for Camus.

Hovering over the novel's composition is Thucydides's account of the plague that swept Athens shortly after the beginning of the war with Sparta. Beyond the dozens of land and sea battles, sieges and pillages that extended across the quarter century of war, it was the plague, Thucydides declared at the start of his work, that caused the greatest suffering.[42] This remarkable assessment deeply impressed Camus. He adopted not just the stages of the event described by the Athenian historian, but adapted Thucydides's austere and ostensibly objective style as well.

Most striking in Thucydides's account of the plague is the speed and force with which it flattened Athenian law and tradition. The institutions of history's greatest democracy, given such eloquent expression by Pericles in his Funeral Oration, collapsed almost immediately under the weight of this unexpected and unprecedented event. Within days, the elaborate stage machinery of Athenian civil and political life seized up, leaving the stage to chaos. Bodies were thrown heedlessly into mass graves, families ignored the pleas of sickened relatives, temples already filled with corpses were still overrun by men and women seeking divine help, and citizens who had concluded that they had been abandoned by the gods now engaged in the most shocking and criminal forms of behavior. In a word, *anomia,* or lawlessness, reigned in Athens—an ancient rendition of the moral and intellectual void that so closely resembles the absurdity of our cosmos.

But *anomia* leeched below and beyond the ramparts of plague-ridden Athens. Liberated from traditional laws and values that now seemed illusory, Athenians embraced what many commentators call political realism, but in fact borders on a form of nihilism. As Victor Davis Hanson remarks, the plague pushed the city beyond a moral threshold: "Once the Athenians had been reduced to such straits, it was nearly impossible to recover their moral bearings in subsequent years."[43] The miserable deaths and horrifying responses inflicted by the plague were just the "lawless precursors," in Hanson's words, to the premeditated and deliberate policies carried out by the "German friend" to whom Camus addressed his wartime letters.

No event better illustrates this moral descent than what, from a strategic perspective, seemed little more than a sideshow. In 416 BCE, an unusually large Athenian naval force landed on Melos, a small island that had, until then, maintained neutrality in the fifteen-year struggle between Athens and Sparta. This was no longer an option, declared the Athenian commanders. Starting today, you are either with us or against us. Choose the former, and you will share the benefits and burdens of an ally; choose the latter, and we will destroy you. The stunned Melians protest the injustice of the ultimatum—to no avail. The Athenians quickly shut them down: "The standard of justice," they reply, "depends on the equality of power to compel and that in fact the strong do what they have the power to do and the weak accept what they have to accept."[44] The Athenians also mock as an "expensive

luxury" the hopes placed by the Melians on the interces-
sion of the gods or Spartans. Once they exhaust all their
arguments, the Melians still refused to surrender. The
Athenians, at home in a cosmos voided of moral principles, conclude: "You seem to us quite unique in your ability to consider the future as something more certain
than what is before your eyes, and to see uncertainties as
realities, simply because you would like them to be so."[45]
They return to their triremes, begin their siege and eventually take the city, killing all the men and enslaving the
women and children.

The events at Melos reflected, moreover, the nihilistic
conviction and brutal efficiency of the German forces
sweeping into what remained of France's "free zone"
while Camus was studying Thucydides at Le Panelier. Is
it possible, when the Athenian envoys tell the Melians
that "your hatred of us is evidence of our power" and
they systematically carry out the ultimatum once they
take Melos—most probably by lining up the Melian prisoners and cutting their throats—Camus was reminded of
the Nazi policy of terror in occupied France? We cannot
know, of course. But it does seem as if Camus, in the first
letter to his "friend," is answering the Athenians as well
as the German: "I cannot believe everything must be sub-
ordinated to a single end. There are means that cannot
be excused."[46]

Among Camus' possessions was a frayed and yellowed
page, apparently torn from a Russian book, framing a

black and white photograph of Ivan Kaliayev. It is more or less a mug shot, taken by the czarist police. A member of the Socialist Revolutionary Party, a radical movement committed to the overthrow of the czarist regime, Kaliayev threw a bomb into a carriage in which the Grand Duke Sergei was traveling in 1905. The explosion propelled in all directions pieces of the victim's body; the perpetrator, who did not try to flee, was hanged a few months later. Kaliayev, whose round and unexceptional face, adorned with a goatee and wool cap, faces the camera with a lucid and calm gaze seems an unlikely hero—a fact perhaps acknowledged by the 1949 production in Paris of Camus' *Les Justes,* or *The Just Assassins,* in which Serge Reggiani, the handsome Italian-French actor, played the assassin.[47]

Upon leaving the Théâtre Hébertot, where the play opened, a critic overheard the sigh of a fellow theatergoer: "Five acts about whether or not one should kill little children."[48] The response to the play, as with Camus' other stage works, was decidedly mixed. Some were deeply moved by the play's depiction of Kaliayev and his fellow revolutionaries as they debated the ethics of killing a man today so that all men and women will know a better tomorrow, while others were frustrated by the characters' lack of psychological depth and their didactic dialogue. Here, as with his other plays, Camus lamented, at times testily, that he had been misunderstood.[49]

His frustration, if not entirely defensible, is nevertheless understandable. There are, no doubt, those who say of *Hamlet:* five acts about whether or not one should kill oneself. Of course, Camus was not Shakespeare, but he never pretended to be. His aim was not to create a psychological portrait, but instead to recreate a historical event and, as did his beloved ancient Greek tragedians, oppose two ethical perspectives of equally compelling force.[50] In the play, Camus pits Kaliayev against a fellow conspirator, Stepan Fedorov, in a fierce struggle over the same question Camus will pose, two years later, at the start of *The Rebel:* can we justify murder?

Kaliayev's position is "Yes, but." Called the "Poet" by his comrades for his questioning and mild manner, he tells Dora, a comrade torn between her duty as a revolutionary and her love for Kaliayev: "Revolution, by all means. But revolution for the sake of life—to give life a chance, if you see what I mean." When Dora replies with the simple truth that they are not giving life, but instead taking it away, Kaliayev tries to explain: "When we kill, we're killing so as to build up a world in which there will be no more killing. We consent to being criminals so that at last the innocent, and only they, will inherit the earth."[51]

But simple consent to become a criminal is not enough, nor is fastidious discrimination in the act of terror. To justify the act of taking the Grand Duke's life, Kaliayev concludes he must also sacrifice his own life. Convinced the czarist state has forced him to become a murderer, Kaliayev tells Dora: "I then remind myself that I'm going to die, too, and everything's all right." The logic of Kaliayev's murderous quid pro quo is clear: by agreeing to die, the "Poet" believes he legitimates his taking of the Grand Duke's life. Perhaps because he is a poet, he seems blissfully unaware of the horrifying flaw in his argument: a life willingly sacrificed is not equal to a life taken of an unwilling victim.

But Dora persists in her doubts, unable to forget that the life they are conspiring to end is precisely that, a life. It is not an abstraction, but instead flesh and blood; it is not a means, but instead the one and only end. "A man is a man," she observes, warning that Kaliayev might discover, as he runs toward the carriage, that perhaps "the Grand Duke has gentle eyes, perhaps you'll see him smiling to himself, scratching his ear. Perhaps—who knows?— you'll see a little scar on his cheek where he cut himself shaving. And, if he looks at you, at that moment..." Groping for an answer, Kaliayev insists he is not killing a man, but despotism, yet quickly recognizes the inadequacy of this reply. All he can hope, he tells Dora, is that his hatred for all that the Grand Duke represents will blind him to the man when the time comes to throw the bomb.

His hatred, we discover, fierce enough to blind him to the Grand Duke, is nevertheless selective. As he runs toward the carriage, coiled to launch the bomb through the window, Kaliayev glimpses two children, the Duke's nephew and niece, sitting across from one another. As he tells his anxiety-worn comrades upon returning to their safe house, the children were "staring into emptiness, and holding themselves very straight. How sad they looked! Dressed up in their best clothes, with their hands resting on their thighs... And everything went with such a rush. Those two serious little faces, and in my hand that hideous weight. I'd have had to throw it at *them*. Like that! Straight at them. No, I just couldn't bring myself..."[52]

But as we learn from Stepan, who listens in growing anger to Kaliayev's story, the children should have been killed, too. Rather than saving the lives of these two children, he shouts, Kaliayev's effort to discriminate between innocent and guilty targets has guaranteed that "thousands of Russian children will go on dying of starvation for years to come.... And to be killed by a bomb is a pleasant death compared to that." As Kaliayev listens in silence, Stepan insists that only when we "stop sentimentalizing about children will the revolution triumph, and we become masters of the world." Kaliayev protests that such logic is no less despotic than the regime they seek to destroy, but it is Dora's scornful reply to Stepan that cuts to the heart of the confrontation: "When that day comes, the revolution will be loathed by the whole human race." The reason for such universal hatred, she continues, is clear: "Even in destruction there's a right way and a wrong way—and there are limits."[53]

When the news arrives that the Grand Duke's carriage will pass again in a few days, Kaliayev gets a second chance. This time, he succeeds: he blows apart the carriage of the Grand Duke, who is traveling alone, then surrenders to the police. All of this cleaves closely to the historical record, as does the visit paid to the jailed Kaliayev by the widowed Grand Duchess. Camus has her tell Kaliayev that she arrived at the scene of her husband's assassination just moments after the bomb had exploded: "I put on a bier all I could collect. What quantities of blood!" With a reflex of either great sadness or even greater sadism, she confides to Kaliayev that, just two hours earlier, her husband was sleeping. "In an armchair with his feet propped up on another chair—as he often did." As for the child Kaliayev had earlier spared, the Grand Duchess reveals she is a heartless brat: "When she's told to give something to poor people, she refuses. She won't go near them."

Quite suddenly, the abstractions of despotism and innocence collapse into the hard and jagged details of everyday life. Shaken at first by the Grand Duchess's revelations—a poor choice of words, in effect, since we already always know that tyrants and children are all too human—Kaliayev reaffirms his faith in the cause for which he killed and will be killed. He implores the Grand Duchess not to seek, as she threatens, a pardon for him; at the end of the play, his comrades learn he walked calmly and unflinchingly to the scaffold. One of his last gestures was to "shake off a fleck of mud that had settled on his shoe"—the act of a man who refused to be a hero, it seems, and instead insisted on remaining a human being.

But does he also shake off his guilt? Has Kaliayev succeeded, by exchanging his life for the Grand Duke's life in order to create a better world, justifying his act of premeditated murder? Inverting the revolutionary's answer, Camus replies "No, but." He rejected the claim that the willingness to lose one's life when taking someone else's life was morally equivalent. Kaliayev's reasoning, Camus wrote, "is false, but respectable."[54]

In a sense, this willingness to die is a necessary, but not sufficient justification to assassinate a tyrant. If political

murder is ever to be legitimate, Camus suggests, other cri-
teria must first be met. Not only must the assassin accept
responsibility and the victim must be a tyrant, but the
act, decided on when there are no alternatives, must be
limited exclusively to the "guilty" party.[55] Innocent lives
must not be taken and the assassin must give up his own
life. What the "scrupulous murderers" of 1905 remind us,
Camus insists, is that "rebellion cannot lead, without
ceasing to be rebellion, to consolation and the comforts of
dogma."[56]

John Foley has rightly suggested that Kaliayev stands
out less by his willingness to die than by his need to entertain doubt. What renders Kaliayev and his comrades
so extraordinary is not their faith in their ends—namely,
a peasantry rescued from misery and servitude, or a nation pulled toward a better future—but instead it is their
persistent doubts over the legitimacy of their means. The
Latin roots of "scrupulous" best describe Kaliayev's stance,
as it does Camus' own moral perspective. For the Romans,
a *scrupulus* was a small and sharp stone that, lodging itself
in one's sandal, makes the act of walking—an activity we
take for granted and never reflect upon—a constant an-
noyance. With every step, our discomfort reminds us we
have just taken a step. Surely, Camus seems to say, a revolutionary committed to killing as a means for a great and
good end must hobble, intellectually and ethically, before and after the act. To kill easily and thoughtlessly—to
lack, like Pucheu, the moral imagination to understand
what happens when you order the deaths of others—is
precisely what Camus most feared. All I wish to do, he

declared, is "refute legitimate murder and assign a clear limit to its demented enterprises."[57]

Greek thought, Camus believed, was based on the idea of limits. "Nothing was carried to extremes, neither religion nor reason, because Greek thought denied nothing, neither reason nor religion. It gave everything its share, balancing light with shade. But the Europe we know, eager for the conquest of totality, is the daughter of excess.... In our madness, we push back the eternal limits, and at once dark Furies swoop down upon us to destroy. Nemesis, goddess of moderation, not of vengeance, is watching. She chastises, ruthlessly, all those who go beyond the limit."[58]

Sophrosyne, the Greek ideal of self-restraint, girds Camus' distinction between rebellion and revolution. Just as self-restraint implies a constant tension between two opposing forces—a straining in two directions at the center of which is the space for creation and progress—the act of rebellion thrives on a similar stress. Whereas Greek epic and tragic poets portrayed this tension through two distinct characters—Penelope and Helen in Homer, Prometheus and Zeus in Aeschylus, or Ajax and Odysseus in Sophocles—Thucydides merges it in a single character, Pericles. More so than any other leader, the Athenian general, according to the historian, was endowed with a mixture of daring and prudence. What he says of Athens in his Funeral Oration was in fact a self-portrait: "We are capable at the same time of taking risks and of estimating them beforehand. Others are brave out of ignorance; and, when they stop to think, they begin to fear. But the man who can most truly be accounted brave is he who best knows the meaning of what is sweet in life and of what is terrible, and then goes out undeterred to meet what is to come."[59]

While Camus never refers to the speech, it nevertheless reflects and perhaps informs his notion of creative tension. The world, for Camus, was a stage for two forms of absurdity: the metaphysical sort, based on the world's refusal to offer meaning to a human race that demands it; and political absurdity, resulting from a state's insistence to give meaning to the unjustifiable suffering it inflicts on its citizens. The rebel, affirms Camus, rejects both kinds of absurdity. She not only says "no" to an unjust ruler, but also says "no" to an unspeaking universe. From his very first step, the rebel "refuses to allow anyone to touch what he is. He is fighting for the integrity of one part of his being. He does not try, primarily, to conquer, but simply to impose." To impose herself on a world empty of meaning: "The rebel does not ask for life, but for reasons for living."[60] But also to impose himself on those who seek to deny his humanity: "He confronts an order of things which oppresses him with the insistence on a kind of right not to be oppressed beyond the limit he can tolerate."[61]

Most critically, however, the rebel seeks to impose a limit on his own self. Rebellion is an act of defense, not offense; it is equipoise, not a mad charge against an opponent. Ultimately, like Weil's notion of attention, it is an active watchfulness in regard to the humanity of others as well as oneself. Just as the absurd never authorizes

despair, much less nihilism, a tyrant's acts never authorizes one to become tyrannical in turn. The rebel does
not deny his master as a fellow human being; he denies
him only as his master. The rebel denies those who have
treated him as less than an equal, but also denies the in-
evitable temptation to dehumanize his former oppressor.
"It is for the sake of everyone in the world that the slave
asserts himself when he comes to the conclusion that a
command has infringed on something in him which does
not belong to him alone, but which is common ground
where all men—even the man who insults and oppresses
him—have a natural community."[62]

Facebook and Twitter, so crucial to the success of the
Arab Spring in 2011, were, in effect, little more than technological means to the oldest of human ends. As Camus
recognized, rebellion invariably moves from individual
to collective response. As he phrased this moment of collective awareness, rebellion plays the same role in our
everyday struggles "as does the 'cogito' in the realm of
thought . . . I rebel—therefore we exist."[63] Camus' state-
ment does not have the logical elegance of Descartes'
formulation, but it resonates with a visceral truth we have
always known: across time and place, rebellion "transcends the individual in so far as it withdraws him from
his supposed solitude and provides him with a reason to
act."[64]

This collective act draws on our admirable qualities,
but it also reveals our tragic condition. Authentic rebellion, in this regard, resembles Periclean Athens: the moment of exquisite balance between daring and caution

cannot last; sooner or later, it will collapse into either tyranny or mediocrity. Thucydides would have undoubtedly recognized his own thoughts in Camus' *pensée de midi,* or noonday thoughts, in which he proposes a "philosophy of limits." Based on the evidence that we cannot know everything, the philosophy concludes that we cannot do anything we please to others. Rebellion, unlike revolution, "aspires to the relative and can only promise an assured dignity coupled with relative justice. It supposes a limit at which the community of man is established."[65] Revolution comes easily, while rebellion "is nothing but pure tension."

Indeed, this tension cannot be maintained indefinitely; sooner or later, ideals will crumble, leaders will grow deluded, followers become disillusioned. Yet, Camus maintains, this tension is as good as it gets for humankind. For the author of *The Rebel,* those who wish to remain in the party of humanity have no choice but to live their lives with this tension. While it is always possible that the end justifies the means, the rebel never fails to reply that the means alone justified the end. Toward the end of his essay, Camus concluded the rebel's logic is "to serve justice so as not to add to the injustice of the human condition, to insist on plain language so as not to increase the universal falsehood, and to wager, in spite of human misery, for happiness." When the book first appeared, this phrase was dismissed as easy grandiloquence disguising an ethical hollowness within. Yet we are now confronted with the truth that there is nothing at all easy, much less hollow, to Camus's claim. Instead, it recognizes the doubts and desperation filling any effort at true rebellion. It demands that we live with provisional outcomes and relative claims, all the while remaining alive to the one absolute: never to allow our rebellion to turn into a revolution.

"In the first days of the revolt you must kill; to shoot down a European is to kill two birds with one stone, to destroy an oppressor and the man he oppresses at the same time: there remains a dead man and a free man; the survivor, for the first time, feels a national soil under his foot." In his preface to Frantz Fanon's *The Wretched of the Earth,* Jean-Paul Sartre made clear that uncontained violence, and not its limits, and absolute certainty, and not doubt, were *du jour.* Published in 1961, a year after Camus—his former friend, since become adversary—died in a car crash, Sartre's exhortation embraced with relish the very "démentes enterprises" that weighed so heavily on the *pied-noir* writer.

Camus would have been shocked, but not surprised by Sartre's defense of those who murdered civilians as a means to national liberation and self-realization. In *The Just Assassins,* Stepan Fedorov had already given voice to this kind of revolution: "There are no limits!" Shortly before the National Liberation Front (FLN) launched its revolt on All Saints Day in 1954, Camus wrote in his notebook: "At the very moment when after so much effort I laid down the limits, believing to be able to reconcile the irreconcilable, the limits burst and I was hurried into a silent unhappiness."[66] Undoubtedly, Camus was describing his state of mind, battered by the intellectual and artistic doubts whipped up by the French Left's critical reaction to *The Rebel*. There was also his increasingly harrowing domestic life, in which he played no small role: his wife Francine suffered repeated bouts of suicidal depression, no doubt deepened by Camus' affair with Maria Casarès, the actress who starred as Dora in the production of *The Just Assassins*.

And yet, wittingly or not, Camus was also brushing a larger canvas whose backdrop was his native Algeria, transformed into an arena for a revolution in which neither side acknowledged the need for limits. By the end of 1956, the moment when Algiers becomes a battlefield between the French Army and the Algerian National Liberation Front, both sides had trampled on and discarded the rules of war. For strategic and tactical reasons, terror became the order of the day for the FLN—a policy aimed, inevitably, at the civilian population. As one of their leaders, Ramdane Abane, observed: "One corpse in a jacket is always worth more than twenty in uniform."[67] The policy was launched on September 30, when bombs planted by FLN operatives exploded at two popular bars in Algiers, killing or maiming dozens of French civilians, including several children. In turn, torture became common practice with the French military whose task was to end the bombings and revolt.[68] The advocates of terrorism and torture both justified their practices as evil but necessary means to good ends; that their respective "good" ends contradicted one another was just the first of many problems.

The Rebel, Camus announced, marked his effort "to confront the reality of the present." After the book's publication, he described it as his taking a "position on current events." By the present, Camus meant the Cold War; by current events, he understood the rise of totalitarianism. As a consequence, the essay's context was a world torn between the liberal democracies of the West and communist regimes of the East. Yet his analysis of revolution held not just for the Soviet Union, but for the FLN as well. Camus had tirelessly denounced the colonialist policies that had transformed the Arabs and Berbers into strangers in their own land: "These people," he warned in 1945, "are not inferior except in regard to the conditions in which they must live, and we have as much to learn from them as they from us. Too many French people in Algeria and elsewhere imagine the Arabs as a shapeless mass without interests."[69] We must stop, he warned his fellow *pieds-noirs,* seeing "the Arabs of Algeria as a bloc, as a nation of murderers. The great majority of them, subjected to every possible ill, have known a kind of distress they alone can express."[70]

But no one was listening. Before he wrapped himself in silence over the mounting horrors of civil war, Camus continued to hammer at the crimes France was committing in its doomed effort to maintain its century-old status quo in Algeria. In the preface to his *Algerian Chronicles,* published in the wake of the Battle of Algiers, Camus is blunt: "Reprisals against the civilian population and the practice of torture are crimes that implicate all of us."

That Frenchmen and women are responsible for such acts "is a humiliation which we must henceforth confront." In the meantime, he declared, "we must refuse any and all justification, even that of efficacy, to these methods." The moment we pretend they can be justified, "neither rules nor values will exist, all causes will be equal and lawless war will consecrate the triumph of nihilism."[71]

To the dismay of erstwhile friends and followers on the French Left, Camus was no kinder to the FLN. While he may have been naive in his conviction that a political solution short of full independence still existed in the 1950s, Camus was prophetic about the future of an FLN-led Algeria. The Arab desire for liberty and equality was just, he affirmed, but the means adopted by the FLN were murderously unjust. Camus' unwavering hostility toward the FLN was fueled by the movement's willingness to use any and all means to achieve its ends. It was not its aim to win independence for Algeria that, for Camus, disqualified the FLN as a representative for the Algerian people. Instead, as David Carroll observes, the "nature of the organization itself and the terrorist campaign it had waged against different civilian populations of Algeria since 1954" blighted its legitimacy.[72]

The FLN's ends, regardless of how desirable—Camus rightly feared a nation condemned to an authoritarian one-party state—could never justify their regime of terror over both *pied-noir* and Arab civilians. What would Kaliayev have done? For Camus, the reply was simple and stark: he and his fellow revolutionaries "would have died—they have given us the proof—rather than lower themselves" to killing innocents.[73] A romantic flourish, perhaps; an impractical principle, probably; the only basis for an ethics worth its name, Mohamed Bouazizi might agree.

EPILOGUE

For much of the 1950s, Camus struggled under the weight of his public reputation. "I am an average man [and] the values that I must defend and illustrate today are average values," he confided to his journal. "It requires such spare talent that I doubt I have it." This reflex of intellectual modesty also surfaced in an interview fated to be Camus' last, given a month before his death. When the interviewer suggested that Camus was a guide for his generation, the response was clear and immediate: "I speak for no one: I have trouble enough finding my own words. I guide no one: I do not know, or know only dimly, where I am going."[1]

No doubt, Camus cultivated his public persona even when he derided or denied his credentials as a public figure. In his private journal, there are more than a few glints of false modesty and vain posturing. Celebrity might have been thrust on him, but Camus was not an accidental public intellectual. As a journalist and editor, novelist and essayist, playwright and director, Camus had consistently sought the public's attention. While he sometimes doubted if he deserved this attention, particularly during the last decade of his life, he was always wounded when others shared those doubts. Sartre's jab at Camus during their slugfest over *The Rebel*—"Your combination of dreary conceit and vulnerability always discouraged people from telling you unvarnished truths"—cut deeply precisely because it contained some truth.[2]

But this does not lessen Camus' stature as a moralist. On the contrary, this flaw has its virtues by bringing him closer to us. As uneasy with himself as others often were with him, Camus frequently cringed upon glimpsing his public portrait. "Virtue is not hateful. But speeches on virtue are. Without a doubt, no mouth in the world, much less mine, can utter them. Likewise, every time somebody interjects to speak of my honesty, there is someone who quivers inside me."[3] There is no reason to doubt the authenticity of such repeated and pained expressions of self-doubt.

Were he alive today, Camus would still quiver. Too many writers—myself included—remind others of the reasons to admire Camus. Were he alive today, Flaubert might add to his *Dictionary of Received Ideas:* "Camus: a good man in dark times." Were he alive today, he might see the ways in which he since had gotten this cause or that event wrong. But we are the ones alive today: a moment's pause reminds us how difficult it was to be right *then,* and how difficult it remains to be right *today* with or, to be sure, against Camus. Camus reminds us of this very point in a letter he wrote to a friend: "One would like to be loved, recognized, for what one is, and by everyone. But that is an adolescent desire. Sooner or later one must get old, agree to be judged, or sentenced, and to receive gifts of love . . . as unmerited. Morality is of no help. Only, truth . . . that is the uninterrupted seeking of it, the decision to tell it when one sees it, on every level, and to live it, gives a meaning, a direction to one's march. But in an era of bad faith, the man who does not want to renounce separating true from false is condemned to a certain kind of exile."[4]

His critics might point out that Camus himself, on more than one occasion, gave us the reasons for his importance. But what of it? Not only had he earned the right, but he had also found the right words. There is little grandiloquence and much that is grand in his Nobel Prize acceptance speech. The writer, Camus declared, must remain faithful not just to her art, but to her fellow men and women as well. The writer "cannot put himself in the service of those who make History; instead, he serves those who endure it. . . . The silence of an unknown prisoner, abandoned and humiliated at the other end of the world, suffices to tear the writer from his exile each time he refuses to forget, in his own life of liberty and privilege, this silence and to broadcast it by means of his art." The nobility of our métier, Camus concluded, "will forever be rooted in two engagements difficult to keep: the refusal to lie about what one knows and the resistance against oppression."

These twin engagements help explain those qualities we traced in this book: Camus's lucidity in recognizing our absurd condition, his attentiveness to the silences of the world and its denizens, his fidelity to our common condition, his insistence on measure when we rebel against those who deny our shared humanity.

Yet they were not his only engagements. At Stockholm, Camus described the artist's predicament: he is caught "between the beauty he cannot do without and the community he cannot tear himself away from." In a word, the world's beauty, and not only its injustices, also demands our attention. Introduced as a writer whose "clear sighted earnestness illuminates the problems of the human conscience," Camus was also earnest in his demurral. "I have never been able to renounce the light," he confessed to the audience, "the pleasure of being, and the freedom in which I grew up."

Like an ocean current, the themes of the beauty and happiness he found in nature flow through Camus' writings. A telling instance is his essay "Return to Tipasa." Camus wrote the essay in 1953—a particularly trying time. Not only had there been the violent quarrel with Sartre over *The Rebel,* but Camus was also dogged by fears that his creative reserves had run dry, leaving him feeling betrayed and becalmed. He flew to Algiers, where he was greeted by several days of rain. But the skies then cleared and Camus drove to Tipasa, overwhelmed by memories of his earlier visits—visits filled with an innocence and confidence he had since lost.

As he climbed toward the Roman ruins, Camus carried the scars of the battles he had fought on behalf of those who could not: starving Berbers, oppressed *pieds-noirs,* tortured resistance fighters, silenced political prisoners. He heard the voices of these "humiliated ones," but he also began to hear "the imperceptible sounds that made up the silence" that had first greeted him: the calls of birds enfolded in bushes, the scrabble of lizards across the hot stones, the whispering of the absinthe plants and "the short, light sighing of the sea" below. Despite his battered lungs, Camus scrambled up the rocky path. As he ascended, he heard "the happy torrents rising within me. It seemed to me that I had at last come to harbor, for a moment at least, and that from now on this moment would never end."[5]

Among the crumbling arches—once the backdrop to his youthful forays with friends—an older and wearier Camus experienced a simple epiphany. "Yes, there is beauty and there are the humiliated. Whatever the difficulties the enterprise may present, I would never like to be unfaithful either to one or the other." Yes, injustice exists, but so too does the sun—the source of measure. Indeed, Camus "*measured* [his] luck, realizing at last that in the worst years of our madness the memory of that sky had never left me. This was what in the end had kept me from despairing. . . . In the middle of winter, I at last discovered that there was in me an invincible summer."[6]

For those who insisted on the purity of political engagement and exigency of moral commitment, Camus' lyrical flights over nature were discomforting. At best they seemed frivolous; at worst, reactionary. Tellingly, George Orwell weathered this same criticism. It is telling because, in part, the many resemblances between the two men are riveting. Both were committed antifascists, but also committed antitotalitarians; both risked their lives in the struggle against fascism (Orwell in Spain, Camus in occupied France); both were journalists and essayists as well as novelists; both men, though despised by many on the European Left, never surrendered their identification with the values of democratic socialism; both men, equally hostile to the imperial policies of their countries, had also lived in the colonies and refused to simplify their complex reality. Of course, both men were also inveterate smokers, tubercular, dead at the age of forty-six, and since hailed, unfortunately, as secular saints.

Yet, ignored by many commentators, both men also insisted on the necessity of beauty. In an essay published shortly after the war, "Some Thoughts on the Common Toad," Orwell dwelt on the abiding and necessary joys of nature. Is it, Orwell asked, "politically reprehensible . . . to point out that life is frequently more worth living because of a blackbird's song, a yellow elm tree in October, or some other natural phenomenon which does not cost money and does not have what the editors of left-wing newspapers call a class angle?" Orwell in fact offers an English equivalent to Camus's "Mediterranean" philosophy—a kind of *pensée de Cotswalds:*

> I think that by retaining one's childhood love of such things as trees, fishes, butterflies and—to return to my first instance—toads, one makes a peaceful and decent future a little more probable, and that by preaching the doctrine that nothing is to be admired except steel and

concrete, one merely makes it a little surer that human beings will have no outlet for their surplus energy except in hatred and leader worship.[7]

Toads do not figure in Camus' childhood, but other mundane marvels did. Sand and sea, light and heat, wind and stars: these were inexhaustible sources of happiness. Camus observed that absurdity might ambush us on a street corner or a sun-blasted beach. But so, too, do beauty and the happiness that attends it. All too often, we know we are happy only when we no longer are. When he shoots the Arab, Meursault wrenches himself from a world with which he had been a piece, and thus at peace. With the pistol's reports, Meursault shatters "the exceptional silence of a beach where [he] had been happy."

Kaliayev also divorces himself from the world; but unlike Meursault, he does so deliberately, fully aware of his sacrifice. Toward the beginning of *The Just Assassins,* Kaliayev and Dora compliment each other's disguises, which they have donned to escape the attention of the czarist police. When Dora tells Kaliayev that his gentlemanly attire suits him, Kaliayev, laughing, returns the compliment, telling Dora how pretty she is in her "fancy dress." But she refuses the compliment: after all, the two friends are planning the assassination of the Grand Duke, an act that will lead to their own deaths. Yet Kaliayev will have none of it: "Dora, there's always such a sad look in your eyes. But you should be gay. . . . There's so much beauty in the world, so much joy."

Near the end of his life, Camus appeared on a television show, *Gros Plan,* to talk about his love of theater. Striding easily down the aisle of the Antoine Theater where he was directing his adaptation of Dostoevsky's *The Possessed,* Camus takes off his trench coat and turns toward the camera. "Today, happiness has become an eccentric activity," he confides with a mischievous smile: "The proof is that we tend to hide from others when we practice it." A pity, he concludes: "As far as I'm concerned, I tend to think that one needs to be strong and happy in order to help those who are unfortunate."[8]

During a visit to Kabylia in late 1937, Camus wrote in his journal: "The demand for happiness and the patient quest for it . . . Be happy with our friends, in harmony with the world, and earn our happiness by following a path which nevertheless leads to death."[9] Happiness, in a word, was a duty as well as a need. To achieve happiness is no simple matter—a truth known to the ancient Epicureans and echoed by Camus. In "Nuptials at Tipasa," Camus declared there is no shame in being happy. But Camus did not confuse happiness with laziness; it is a state we achieve neither through distraction nor entertainment, but instead through attention and effort. "It is not so easy to become what one is," he warned in the same essay, "to rediscover one's deepest measure."[10]

When he returned to Tipasa fifteen years later, no longer an obscure writer living in straitened circumstances, but a celebrated and controversial intellectual, Camus once again took his own measure. Political engagements had taken a tremendous toll, and Tipasa recalled other demands for Camus. "Forsaking beauty and the sensual happiness attached to it and exclusively serving misfortune," he concluded, "calls for a nobility I lack."[11] Of course, what Camus reaffirms is not sensual needs against moral deeds, but instead the necessary balance between the two. Measure, in a word. For Camus, true nobility lies in lucid acceptance of the world, its beauties and its limits, its joys and its demands, its inhabitants and our common lot.

Ever since the ancient Greeks, we have felt that a bond exists between justice and beauty—or, expressed with less concision, but greater precision, between the state of equality among human beings and the level of symmetry between objects. Distributive justice and beauty, the philosopher Stuart Hampshire once remarked, share, if only analogically, "balance and the weighing of both sides."[12] This common ground, however, may have foundations that lie deeper than simple analogy. Elaine Scarry writes, in a deeply Camusian essay, that our fierce attraction toward symmetry, or beauty, drives our passion for equality; our grounding in a world whose perceived beauty rests on balance and symmetry makes us thirst for political and social justice. For those human communities "too young to have yet had time to create justice, as well as in periods when justice has been taken away, beautiful things... hold steadily visible the manifest good of equality and balance."[13] Not just visible, but indivisible: we understand, if only obscurely, that life where one, but not the other existed, is a life unfulfilled.

Moreover, beauty defeats, if only for short moments, the selfish concerns and preoccupations that mostly govern our lives. Filled with wonder, or filled with love, we forget ourselves—a precondition for making room for others. For Simone Weil, this was the work of attention: in order to truly see, to open ourselves to beauty and justice, we must suspend our thought, "leaving it detached, empty and ready to be penetrated by the object."[14] The moments among the ruins at Tipasa, stretched on the sand of an Algiers beach, climbing the mountains of Kabylia, moments when he was alone and silence reigned, were moments for Camus when his dedication to the cause of justice was again justified.

In an early essay, "Between Yes and No," written when he had little more than a university diploma in hand and no job in sight, Camus observed: "When we are stripped down to a certain point, nothing leads anywhere any more, hope and despair are equally groundless, and the whole of life can be summed up in an image."[15]

Perhaps for those born with no memories of the first half of the twentieth century, the image will be in black and white. This is certainly the case for Camus. The best-known images of Camus, of course, are black and white. Upturned trench coat collar and cigarette caught between his lips or fingers; sitting behind a desk or leaning against a wall, reading a newspaper; staring intently at a friend or lover, the lines of his face either furrowed or smiling.

In a way, these black-and-white images are apt. For the photographer Robert Frank, these were the only colors of photography. "To me they symbolize the alternatives of hope and despair to which mankind is forever subjected." Camus might have agreed, reminding us all the while that while we have no reason to hope, we must also never despair. But the image he would want us to take away, perhaps, is not a black-and-white shot captured by Cartier-Bresson. Instead, it is a scarcely known photograph, taken for a French weekly magazine, of Camus and his close friend Michel Gallimard not long before the car crash that took their lives. In a portrait awash in Mediterranean colors, the two men are sitting at a café terrace at a table covered with plates and bottles. Gallimard, wearing a reddish stubble and shy smile, seems in mid-sentence, while Camus, one arm over his friend's shoulder, the other poised under his chin, looks slightly to the camera's right, his sun-tanned face alight with a broad smile. Gazing at the portrait, a line from "Nuptials at Tipasa" surges into my thoughts: "Everything here leaves me intact, I surrender nothing of myself, and don no mask: learning patiently and arduously how to live is enough for me."[16]

Camus's pen, not a camera, gives us a second, no less vividly colored image. It occurs in *The First Man,* enfolded in a chapter where Camus recollects the games he played as a child in Algiers. On windy days at school, he and his friends gathered palm branches, rushed to the school's terrace that overlooked the desert plains, and faced the wind while gripping the branches. "The branch would immediately be plastered against him," Camus remembers, while he breathed "its smell of dust and straw." The winner of the contest, he notes, "was the one who first reached the end of the terrace without letting the wind tear the branch from his hands, then he would stand erect holding the palm branch at arm's length . . . struggling victoriously for as long as possible against the raging force of the wind."[17]

With this as the image I will always imagine Camus happy.

NOTES

PROLOGUE

1. Albert Camus, *Notebooks 1951–1959,* trans. Ryan Bloom (Chicago: Ivan Dee, 2008), 31.
2. Albert Camus, *Lyrical and Critical Essays,* trans. Ellen Kennedy (New York: Knopf, 1968), 66.
3. Ibid., 164–165.
4. Ibid., 168–169.
5. See, for example, *Le Figaro*, December 5, 2007.
6. The French press was awash with accounts of the affair, beginning in late November 2009. See, for example, "Le fils d'Albert Camus refuse le transfert de son père au Panthéon," *Le Monde,* November 21, 2009.
7. The summer of 2012 has witnessed yet another contest over Camus' legacy. Plans for the grand centenary celebration in Aix-en-Provence collapsed when the city of Aix and Catherine Camus fell out over the nature of the exhibits. The city's mayor, who represents a large community of *pieds-noirs* who resettled in Aix after 1962, disliked the original curator, the

historian Benjamin Stora, whose work is very critical of the politics of the French Algerian community. The subsequent nomination of the philosopher Michel Onfray to the post of curator also fell to political controversy when the Socialist government, which supported Stora, refused to subsidize it.

8. Alix de Saint-André, *Papa est au Panthéon* (Paris: Gallimard, 2001), 92.

9. Assia Djebar, *Le Blanc de l'Algérie* (Paris: Albin Michel, 1995).

10. Djemaï Abdelkader, "J'ai grandi au milieu des clochers," *Le Monde,* December 17, 2009.

11. As for Camus' private life, admirers have mostly avoided discussion of his many extramarital affairs, most famously with the actress Maria Casarès, which undoubtedly played a role in his wife's repeated clinical depressions and attempted suicides. For example, Michel Onfray's recent account fobs off responsibility on Francine Camus for her repeated depressions, concluding that her family's accusations against Camus made him into "an easy scapegoat." See his *L'Ordre libertaire: La vie philosophique d'Albert Camus* (Paris: Flammarion, 2012), 478. Another recent biographer, Elizabeth Hawes, offers a far more nuanced and insightful portrait of Camus and the women in his life. See *Camus: A Romance* (New York: Grove Press, 2009), 213-228.

12. Hawes, *Camus: A Romance,* 217.

13. Tony Judt, *The Burden of Responsibility* (Chicago: University of Chicago Press, 1998), 25.

14. Ibid., 122.

15. Camus, *Lyrical and Critical Essays,* 160-161.

16. *The Myth of Sisyphus and Other Essays,* trans. Justin O'Brien (New York: Vintage 1991), 3.

17. *The Oresteia*, trans. Robert Fagles (New York: Penguin, 1975), 109.

18. Martha Nussbaum, *The Fragility of Goodness* (Cambridge: Cambridge University Press, 1986), 45.

19. Ibid., 49–150.

20. Camus, *Lyrical and Critical Essays*, 169.

1. ABSURDITY

1. Albert Camus, *Essais*, ed. Roger Quilliot (Paris: Gallimard, 1965), 99.

2. Oliver Todd, *Albert Camus: Une Vie* (Paris: Gallimard, 1996), 281.

3. Albert Camus, *The Myth of Sisyphus and Other Essays*, trans. Justin O'Brien (New York: Vintage, 1991), 6.

4. Camus, *Essais*, 100.

5. Robert Solomon, *Dark Feelings, Grim Thoughts* (New York: Oxford University Press, 2006), 37.

6. Thomas Nagel, *The View from Nowhere* (New York: Oxford University Press, 1986), 214.

7. Camus, *The Myth of Sisyphus*, 2.

8. Quoted in Sarah Bakewell, *How to Live: Or, A Life of Montaigne* (New York: Other Press, 2010), 37.

9. Camus, *The Myth of Sisyphus*, 21.

10. Ibid., 39.

11. Ibid., 41.

12. Ibid., 80.

13. Ibid., 53.

14. Albert Camus, *Notebooks: 1935–1951*, trans. Philip Thody and Justin O'Brien (New York: Marlowe and Co., 1998), 27.

15. Letter from Albert Camus to Jean Grenier, February 2, 1939, in *Albert Camus and Jean Grenier: Correspondence, 1932–1960*, trans. Jan F. Rigaud (Lincoln: University of Nebraska Press, 2003), 20.

16. Camus, *Essais*, 1417–22.

17. Todd, *Camus*, 252.

18. Ibid., 214.

19. Albert Camus, *Le Soir républicain*, November 6, 1939, re-printed in *Essais*, 1380.

20. Camus, *Notebooks*, 151–152.

21. Camus, *Le Soir républicain*, November 6, 1939, reprinted in *Essais*, 1378, 1380.

22. Camus, *Notebooks*, 179, 175.

23. For a general background, see Alan Riding, *And the Show Went On* (New York: Knopf, 2010).

24. Alistaire Horne, *The Fall of France* (New York: Penguin, 1977) offers a solid account of these events.

25. Camille Bourniquel, quoted in Hanna Diamond, *Fleeing Hitler: France 1940* (Oxford: Oxford University Press, 2007), 2.

26. Albert Camus, *The Rebel*, trans. Anthony Bower (New York: Vintage, 1991), 4.

27. In part because of the book's widespread use in the nation's schools, about 130,000 copies of *L'Etranger* are sold every year in France. See "Le Choc des Titans," at *Marianne* www.marianne.net/Le-choc-des-Titans_a225070.html.

28. Albert Camus, *The Stranger*, trans. Matthew Ward (New York: Vintage, 1989), 24.

29. Ibid., 35.

30. Ibid., 59.

31. Jean-Jacques Rousseau, "Discourse on the Origin and Foundations of Inequality Among Men," in *The First and Second Discourses*, trans. Roger Masters and Judith Masters (New York: St. Martin's Press, 1964), 117.

32. Camus, *The Stranger*, 97, 80.

33. Todd, *Camus*, 253.

34. Quoted in Todd, *Camus*, 256.

35. Camus, *The Myth of Sisyphus,* 30.
36. Albert Camus, *The First Man,* trans. David Hapgood (New York: Knopf, 1995), 95-96, 268.
37. Camus, *The Myth of Sisyphus,* v.
38. Ibid., 12.
39. Ibid., 14.
40. Camus, *Notebooks,* 182.
41. Henry Bordeaux, quoted in Richard Vinen, *The Unfree French* (New Haven: Yale University Press, 2007), 54.
42. Quoted in Todd, *Camus,* 259-260.
43. Camus, *Notebooks,* 182-183.
44. Camus, *The Myth of Sisyphus,* 138.
45. See Robert Graves, *The Greek Myths* (Penguin: New York, 1975), vol. 1, 216-220.
46. Camus, *The Myth of Sisyphus,* 130.
47. Ibid., 119.
48. See the R.G. Bury translation and J. Garrett commentary of the text at http://people.wku.edu/jan.garrett/302/critias.htm
49. Homer, *The Iliad,* trans. Robert Fitzgerald (New York: Anchor, 1987), Bk. 6, ll.168-173.
50. Camus, *Notebooks,* 186.
51. "The Minotaur, Or the Stop in Oran," in *The Myth of Sisyphus and Other Essays,* 165.
52. Todd, *Camus,* 271.
53. Herbert Lottman, *Albert Camus* (Corte Madera, CA: Gingko Press, 1997), 254.
54. Camus, *Notebooks,* 189.
55. Camus, *The Myth of Sisyphus,* 119.
56. Richard Taylor emphasizes this point in his essay "The Meaning of Life," in *The Meaning of Life,* ed. E. D. Klemke (New York: Oxford University Press, 1981), 141-150.

57. Ibid., 148.

58. Lottman, *Camus,* 272.

59. Letter to Christiane Galindo, quoted in Todd, *Camus,* 303; Camus, *Notebooks,* 23.

60. Camus, *Notebooks,* 24.

61. Ibid., 25.

62. Ibid.

63. Camus, *The Myth of Sisyphus,* 27.

64. Albert Camus, *Oeuvres Complètes,* ed., Jacqueline Levi-Valensi (Paris: Gallimard, 2008), vol. 1, 1259.

65. Quoted in Todd, *Camus,* 304.

66. Ibid., 308.

67. Jean-Paul Sartre, "A Commentary on *The Stranger,*" in *Existentialism Is a Humanism,* trans. Carol Macomber (New Haven: Yale University Press, 2007), 78–79.

68. Camus, *The Myth of Sisyphus,* 15.

69. Colin Wilson, *Anti-Sartre* (London: Borgos Press, 1981), 10.

70. Sartre, "A Commentary on *The Stranger,*" 90–91.

71. Camus, *The Stranger,* 101.

72. Ibid., 122.

73. Stendhal, *Scarlet and Black,* trans. Margaret Shaw (New York: Penguin, 1953), 502.

74. Taylor, "The Meaning of Life," 32.

75. A. J. Ayer, "Albert Camus," *Horizon* 13 (1946): 159.

76. Ibid., 168.

77. Ibid., 160.

78. A. J. Ayer, *Part of My Life* (New York: Harcourt, Brace, Jovanovich, 1977), 284.

79. Thomas Nagel, "The Absurd," *Journal of Philosophy* 63, no.20 (1971): 716.

80. Nagel, "The Absurd," 718.

81. Ibid.

82. Ibid., 720.

83. Ibid., 722.

84. Ibid., 727.

85. Taylor, "The Meaning of Life," 102.

86. Jeffrey Gordon, "Nagel or Camus on the Absurd?" *Philosophy and Phenomenological Research* 45, no.1 (1984): 16.

87. Camus, *The Myth of Sisyphus,* 55.

88. Solomon, *Dark Feelings, Grim Thoughts,* 45.

89. Iris Murdoch, *The Sovereignity of Good* (London: Routledge, 1970), 65.

90. See Robert Alter, *The Wisdom Books* (New York: Vintage, 2011), passim.

91. Quoted in Jennifer Hecht, *Doubt: A History* (New York: Harper, 2004), 71.

92. Jack Miles, *God: A Biography* (New York: Vintage, 1994), 11.

93. Patrick Gerard Henry, *We Only Know Men* (Washington, DC: Catholic University Press, 2007), 113.

94. Camus, *Notebooks,* 42.

95. Camus, *The Myth of Sisyphus,* vi.

96. Camus, *Notebooks,* 24.

97. Philip Haillie, *Lest Innocent Blood Be Shed* (New York: Harper, 1994), 103.

98. Camus, *Notebooks,* 93.

2. SILENCE

1. *The Confessions of Saint Augustine*, trans. Rex Warner (New York: Penguin, 1963), 20.

2. Albert Camus, *The First Man* (New York: Knopf, 1994), trans. David Hapgood, 27.

3. Max Picard, *The World of Silence*, trans. Stanley Godman (Chicago: Henry Regnery, 1952), 1.

4. Camus, *The First Man,* 98.

5. Ibid., 97.

6. Albert Camus, "Between Yes and No," in *Lyrical and Critical Essays*, trans. Ellen Kennedy (New York: Knopf, 1968), 32, 38.

7. Ibid., 33–34.

8. "Preface to the Wrong and the Right Side," in *Lyrical and Critical Essays*, 16.

9. Camus, *The First Man*, 300.

10. Albert Camus, *Oeuvres complètes*, vol.1, ed. Jacqueline Lèvi-Valensi(Paris: Gallimard, 2006), 1436.

11. Ibid., 1098.

12. Albert Camus, "Le Vent à Djémila," in *Oeuvres complètes*, 1:111.

13. Ibid., 112.

14. Ibid.

15. Stuart Sim, *Manifesto for Silence* (Edinburgh: Edinburgh University Press, 2007), 39.

16. Albert Camus, "Summer in Algiers," in *Lyrical and Critical Essays*, 90.

17. *Cahiers Albert Camus 3: Fragments d'un combat: 1938–1940*, vol.1, ed. Jacqueline Lévi-Valensi (Paris: Gallimard, 1978), 288. The recently published fourth volume of Camus' writings in Pléiade, which contains his Algerian writings, does not include articles found in this earlier collection. The reference to Berber companions is in Patrick McCarthy, *Camus* (New York: Random House, 1982), 118.

18. Camus, *Fragments d'un combat*, 1:289.

19. Albert Camus, *Essais*, ed. Roger Quilliot (Paris: Gallimard, 1965), 910.

20. Ibid., 915.

21. Camus, *Fragments d'un combat*, 1:288.

22. Ibid., 314.

23. Ibid., 335–336.

24. Ibid., 300.

25. Camus, *The First Man*, 186.
26. Ibid., 192–193.
27. Albert Camus, *Notebooks 1951–1959*, trans. Ryan Bloom (Chicago: Ivan Dee, 2008), 20.
28. Albert Camus, *The Rebel*, trans. Anthony Bower (New York: Vintage, 1992), 236.
29. Quoted in John Foley, *Albert Camus: From the Absurd to Revolt* (Montreal: McGill-Queen's University Press, 2008), 117.
30. Ibid.
31. Camus, *Notebooks: 1951–1959*, 51.
32. Ibid., 50.
33. Ibid., 56–57.
34. Ibid., 40.
35. Albert Camus, *Exile and the Kingdom*, trans. Carol Cosman (New York: Vintage, 2007), 50.
36. Ibid., 52.
37. Ibid., 60.
38. Ibid.
39. Olivier Todd, *Camus: Une Vie* (Paris: Gallimard, 1996), 346.
40. Vercors, *The Silence of the Sea*, trans. Cyril Connolly (New York: Berg, 1991), 74.
41. Picard, *World of Silence*, 13.
42. Camus, *Oeuvres complètes*, 4:1358.
43. Camus, *Exile and the Kingdom*, 65.
44. Camus, *Oeuvres complètes*, 4:372.
45. Ibid., 4:375.
46. Ibid., 4:376.
47. Quoted in Todd, *Camus*, 633.
48. *Le Monde*, 14 décembre 1957, reprinted in Camus, *Essais*, 1881–1882.
49. Camus, *Oeuvres Complètes* 4:1405-6. I am guilty of having relied on this mistranslation in my previous book on Camus.

50. Albert Camus, "Letters to a German Friend," in *Resistance, Rebellion and Death,* trans. Justin O'Brien (New York: Knopf, 1963), 21.

51. Camus, "Between Yes and No," 37-38.

52. Camus, *Lyrical and Critical Essays,* 169-170.

53. Camus, *Essais,* 1490.

54. Albert Camus, *The Myth of Sisyphus,* trans. Justin O'Brien (New York: Vintage, 1991), 137.

55. Camus, *The Rebel,* 66.

56. Michel Onfray, *L'Ordre Libertaire: La vie philosophique d'Albert Camus* (Paris: Flammarion, 2012), 68.

57. Camus, *The Rebel,* 76.

58. Friedrich Nietzsche, *The Gay Science,* trans. Walter Kaufman (New York: Vintage, 1974), 272.

59. Camus, *Notebooks 1951–1959,* 116.

60. The photo is reproduced in Catherine Camus, ed., *Albert Camus: Solitaire et solidaire* (Paris: Lafon, 2009), 30.

61. Erich Heller, *The Importance of Nietzsche* (Chicago: University of Chicago Press, 1988), 184.

62. Camus, *Notebooks 1951–1959,* 176.

63. Ibid., 243.

3. MEASURE

1. Albert Camus, *The Rebel,* trans. Anthony Bower (New York: Vintage, 1991), 300.

2. Quoted in Ronald Aronson, *Camus and Sartre: The Story of a Friendship and the Quarrel that Ended It* (Chicago: University of Chicago Press, 2004), 147.

3. Albert Camus, *Notebooks: 1935–1951,* trans. Philip Thody and Justin O'Brien (New York: Marlowe and Co., 1998), 13.

4. Camus, *The Rebel,* 306. Camus first presents this sentiment in his essay "Helen's Exile," published in 1948. "Ulysses, on

Calypso's island, is given the choice between immortality and the land of his fathers. He chooses this earth, and death with it." (Albert Camus, *Lyrical and Critical Essays,* trans. Ellen Kennedy [New York: Knopf, 1968], 152.)

5. Paul Archambault, *Camus' Hellenic Sources* (Chapel Hill: University of North Carolina Press, 1972), 11.

6. Quoted in Bernard Williams, *Shame and Necessity* (Berkeley: University of California Press, 1993), 19.

7. Albert Camus, "Prometheus in the Underworld," in *Lyrical and Critical Essays,* 141.

8. Quoted in Herbert Lottman, *Albert Camus* (Madera, CA: Gingko Press, 1997), 101.

9. Camus, *Notebooks 1935–1951,* 84.

10. Ibid., 85.

11. Albert Camus, "Nuptials at Tipasa," in *Lyrical and Critical Essays,* 67.

12. Ibid., 68.

13. As Gérard Crespo points out, Audisio was appalled by the "Algerianist" literary movement, which under the influence of Italian Fascism (as well as French *fascisant* writers like Charles Maurras), yoked the spirit of the Mediterranean to the ancient Roman empire and elided the history of Muslim and Arab Africa. See his "Camus, Audisio et la Méditerranée," in *Albert Camus et la pensée du Midi,* ed. Jean-François Mattéi (Nice: Editions Ovadia, 2008), 123–134. See also Peter Dunwoodie, "From *Noces* to *L'Etranger,*" in *The Cambridge Companion to Camus,* ed. Edward Hughes (Cambridge: Cambridge University Press, 2007), 147–164.

14. Albert Camus, "The New Mediterranean Culture," in *Lyrical and Critical Essays,* 191.

15. Conor Cruise O'Brien, *Albert Camus of Europe and Africa* (New York: Viking, 1970), 9.

16. Neil Foxlee, *"The New Mediterranean Culture": A Text and Its Contexts* (Bern: Peter Lang, 2010).

17. See Lottman, *Camus,* 59.

18. Albert Camus, *Cahiers Albert Camus 3: Fragments d'un combat, 1938–1940* v.1, ed. Jacqueline Lévi-Valensi (Paris: Gallimard, 1978), 278–279.

19. Ibid., 289.

20. Ibid., 288.

21. Lottman, *Camus,* 59.

22. Camus, "Prometheus in the Underworld," 138–139.

23. Ibid., 139.

24. Ibid., 140.

25. Lottman, *Camus,* 645.

26. Olivier Todd, *Albert Camus: Une vie* (Paris: Gallimard, 1996), 525.

27. Lottman, *Camus,* 395.

28. Simone Weil, "The Iliad, or the Poem of Force," in *Simone Weil: An Anthology,* ed. Sian Miles (New York: Weidenfeld and Nicolson, 1986), 171.

29. Ibid., 175.

30. Ibid.

31. Williams, *Shame and Necessity,* 151.

32. Albert Camus, *The Plague,* trans., Stuart Gilbert (New York: Vintage, 1991), 127.

33. Albert Camus, *Camus at Combat,* ed. Jacqueline Lévi-Valensi (Princeton: Princeton University Press, 2006), 205, 200.

34. Ibid.

35. Ibid.

36. Ibid., 216.

37. Ibid.

38. Albert Camus, "On the Future of Tragedy," in *Lyrical and Critical Essays,* 310.

39. Ibid.

40. Albert Camus, "L'Algèrie déchirée," in *Essais,* ed. Roger Quilliot (Paris: Gallimard, 1965), 985.

41. Philippe Vanney, "Sur l'idée de trêve dans l'oeuvre politique d'Albert Camus," in *Albert Camus: Les Extremes et l'équilibre,* ed. David Walker (Amsterdam: Rodopi, 1994), 115–128.

42. Albert Camus, "Appeal for a Civilian Truce," in *Resistance, Rebellion, Death,* trans. Justin O'Brien (New York: Knopf, 1963), 131.

43. Aurelain Craiutu, *A Virtue for Courageous Minds: Moderation in French Political Thought, 1748–1830* (Princeton: Princeton University Press, 2012), 15.

44. Ibid., 21.

45. In the most recent large study of Camus' life and thought, the French philosopher Michel Onfray emphasizes these repeated claims by Camus, all the while insisting he was a philosopher in the sense understood by the ancient schools of philosophy: that philosophy was a guide to living one's life. Michel Onfray, *L'Ordre Libertaire: La vie philosophique d'Albert Camus* (Paris: Flammarion, 2012).

46. Archambault, *Camus' Hellenic Sources,* 44.

47. Martha Nussbaum, *The Fragility of Goodness* (Cambridge: Cambridge University Press, 1986), 32.

48. Ibid.

49. Ibid., 50.

50. Aeschylus, *Seven Against Thebes,* trans. Anthony Hecht and Helen Bacon (Oxford: Oxford University Press, 1973), 67.

51. Quoted in David Carroll, *Albert Camus the Algerian* (New York: Columbia University Press, 2007), 137–138.

52. Camus, *The Rebel,* 27.

53. Nussbaum, *The Fragility of Goodness,* 45.

4. FIDELITY

1. Albert Camus, *The First Man,* trans. David Hapgood (New York: Knopf, 1994), 64–66.
2. Ibid., 82.
3. Albert Camus, "Reflections on the Guillotine," in *Resistance, Rebellion and Death,* trans. Justin O'Brien (New York: Knopf, 1963), 132.
4. André Comte-Sponville, *Petit traité des grandes vertues* (Paris: PUF, 1995), 28.
5. Ibid., 30.
6. Albert Camus, *Actuelles II, Ouevres complètes,* vol. 2 (Paris: Gallimard, 2008), 401.
7. Albert Camus, "Letters to a German Friend," in *Resistance, Rebellion and Death,* trans. O'Brien, 7.
8. Ibid., 21.
9. Albert Camus, *Camus at Combat,* ed. Jacqueline Lévi-Valensi (Princeton: Princeton University Press, 2007), 4.
10. Ibid., 6.
11. Comte-Sponville, *Petit traité des grandes vertues,* 29.
12. Camus, "Letters to a German Friend," 24.
13. Comte-Sponville, *Petit traité des grandes vertues,* 29
14. Camus, *Ouevres complètes,* 2:402.
15. Albert Camus, *Notebooks: 1935–1951,* trans. Philip Thody and Justin O'Brien (New York: Marlowe and Co., 1998), 202.
16. Olivier Todd, *Albert Camus: Une Vie* (Paris: Gallimard, 1996), 507.
17. Michele de Montaigne, *The Complete Essays of Montaigne,* trans. Donald Frame (Palo Alto: Stanford University Press, 1958), 60–62.
18. Ibid., 323.
19. See Sarah Bakewell, *How to Live: Or, a Life of Montaigne* (New York: Other Press, 2010), 205.

20. Montaigne, *Essays*, 315–316.

21. Henri Alleg, *The Question*, trans. John Calder (Lincoln: University of Nebraska Press, 2006), 44.

22. Ibid., 34.

23. Or nearly unique: General Jacques Massu also chose to undergo torture for the same reasons as Bigeard. Remarkably, in 2001, in the wake of the revelation made in *Le Monde* by Louisette Ighilahriz, who was tortured by Massu's men, Massu not only apologized publicly, but also admitted that torture was never "indispensable."

24. Quoted by Agnès Spiquel and Philippe Vanney, "Notice," in *Ouevres complètes*, 4:1415.

25. Simone de Beauvoir, *The Force of Circumstance*, trans. Richard Howard (New York: Putnam, 1965), 391–392, 396.

26. Quoted in Ronald Aronson, *Camus and Sartre: The Story of a Friendship and the Quarrel that Ended It* (Chicago: University of Chicago Press, 2004), 211.

27. Montaigne, *Essays*, 324.

28. Ibid., 313.

29. Ibid., 518.

30. Ibid., 600–601.

31. Camus, *Ouevres complètes*, 4:298.

32. Albert Camus, *Notebooks 1951–1959*, trans. Ryan Bloom (Chicago: Ivan Dee, 2008), 68.

33. Alleg, *The Question*, xvi.

34. Camus, *Ouevres complètes*, 3:1025.

35. Ibid.4:299.

36. Ibid., 363.

37. Albert Camus, *Notebooks 1951–1959* trans. Ryan Bloom (Chicago: Ivan Dee, 2008), 144.

38. Camus, *Notebooks 1951–1959*, 58.

39. Camus, "Reflections," 133.

40. Eve Morisi, ed., *Albert Camus contre la peine de mort* (Paris: Gallimard, 2011).

41. Ibid., 244.

42. Ibid., 246.

43. *Albert Camus and Jean Grenier: Correspondence 1932–1960*, trans. Jan Rigaud (Lincoln: University of Nebraska Press, 1981), 112.

44. Elaine Scarry, *The Body in Pain* (Oxford: Oxford University Press, 1985), 29.

45. Ibid., 4–5.

46. Camus, *Notebooks 1935–1951*, 182.

47. Camus, *Camus at* Combat, 258–259.

48. Ibid., 260.

49. Camus, "Reflections," 137.

50. Camus, *Ouevres complètes*, 4:129.

51. Ibid., 141.

52. Ibid., 155.

53. Ibid., 131.

54. Ibid., 135.

55. Albert Camus, *Essais,* ed. Rogert Quilliot (Paris: Gallimard, 1965), 1469.

56. Ibid.

57. Ibid., 1470.

58. Camus, *Camus at* Combat, 20–21.

59. Camus, *Essais,* 1469.

60. Camus, *Camus at* Combat, 165.

61. Ibid., 168–169.

62. Todd, *Camus,* 374.

63. Morisi, *Albert Camus contre la peine de mort,* 195–196.

64. Gisèle Halimi, *Le Lait d'orager* (Paris: Pocket, 2001), 181.

65. Morisi, *Albert Camus contre la peine de mort,* 197–198.

66. Ibid., 201–202.

67. Ibid., 204.

68. Albert Camus, *Cahiers Albert Camus 3: Fragments d'un combat, 1938–1940*, ed. Jacqueline Lévi-Valensi (Paris: Gallimard, 1978), v.2, 368.

69. Morisi, *Albert Camus contre la peine de mort*, 205.

70. Halimi, *Le Lait d'orager*, 177.

71. See, for example, Herbert Lottman, *Albert Camus* (Madera, CA: Gingko Press, 1997), 652–653.

72. Camus, *The First Man*, 27.

73. Ibid., 61.

5. REVOLT

1. Albert Camus, *The Myth of Sisyphus*, trans. Justin O'Brien (New York: Vintage, 1991), 55.

2. Tahar Ben Jelloun, *Par le feu* (Paris: Gallimard, 2011).

3. Akram Belkaïd, "Mohamed Bouazizi parle encore aux Tunisiens," *Slate Afrique*, December 18, 2011.

4. Albert Camus, *The Rebel*, trans. Anthony Bower (New York: Vintage, 1991), 10.

5. Ibid., 3-4.

6. Ibid., 3.

7. Albert Camus, *Camus at Combat*, ed. Jacqueline Lévi-Valensi (Princeton: Princeton University Press, 2007), 259.

8. Ibid., 236–237.

9. Quoted in John Foley, *Albert Camus* (Montreal: McGill-Queen's Press, 2008), 39.

10. Maurice Merleau-Ponty, *Humanism and Terror* (Boston: Beacon Press, 1969), 153.

11. For an account of the confrontation, see Olivier Todd, *Albert Camus: Une Vie* (Paris: Gallimard, 1996), 445–446.

12. Albert Camus, *Essais*, ed. Rogert Quilliot (Paris: Gallimard, 1965), 355–356.

13. Quoted in Robert Solomon, *Dark Feelings, Grim Thoughts* (Oxford: Oxford University Press, 2006), 189.

14. Camus, *The Rebel,* 10.

15. Hannah Arendt, *Between Past and Future* (New York: Penguin, 2006), 78.

16. Camus, *The Rebel,* 207.

17. Ibid., 226.

18. Camus, *Camus at* Combat, 42.

19. John Sweets, *The Politics of Resistance in France, 1940–1944* (DeKalb: Northern Illinois University Press, 1976), 218.

20. For the text in full, see http://blogs.mediapart.fr/mot-cle /conseil-national-de-la-resistance/.

21. Albert Camus, *Oeuvres complètes,* vol. 3, ed. Raymond Gay-Crosier (Paris: Gallimard, 2008), 1099.

22. Camus, *Camus at* Combat, 55.

23. Michel Onfray, *L'Ordre Libertaire: La vie philosophique d'Albert Camus* (Paris: Flammarion, 2012), 317.

24. Camus, *Essais,* 357.

25. Camus, *Camus at* Combat, 107.

26. Ibid., 267.

27. Albert Camus, *American Journals,* trans. Hugh Levick (New York: Paragon House, 1987), 51.

28. Ibid., 42.

29. Ibid.

30. Ibid., 49.

31. Elizabeth Hawes, *Camus, a Romance* (New York: Grove Press, 2009), 101.

32. Camus, *American Journals,* 49.

33. Camus, *The Rebel,* 206.

34. Ibid., 205.

35. Tony Judt, *The Burden of Responsibility* (Chicago: University of Chicago Press, 1998), 116.

36. Ibid., 104.

37. Camus, *Camus at* Combat, 260–261.

38. Roberto Calasso, *The Marriage of Cadmus and Harmony* (New York: Knopf, 1993), 125.

39. Herodotus, *The History,* trans. David Grene (Chicago: University of Chicago Press, 1987), 472.

40. Camus, *The Rebel,* 27.

41. Camus, *Notebooks 1935–1951,* trans. Philip Thody (New York: Marlowe & Co, 1998), 193.

42. Thucydides, *History of the Peloponnesian War,* trans. Rex Warner (New York: Penguin, 1988), 48.

43. Victor Davis Hanson, *A War Like No Other* (New York: Random House, 2005), 77–78.

44. Thucydides, *History of the Peloponnesian War,* 402.

45. Ibid., 407.

46. Albert Camus, *Resistance, Rebellion and Death,* trans. Justin O'Brien (New York: Knopf, 1963), 3–4.

47. See Catherine Camus, ed., *Albert Camus: Solitaire et solidaire* (Paris: Lafon, 2009), 122–125.

48. The critic was the writer (and friend of Camus) Nicola Chiaromonte. See Hebert Lottman, *Albert Camus* (Madera, CA: Gingko Press, 1997), 502.

49. According to Christine Margerisson, the "reception of [Camus'] plays seem to have caused a rift between him and his audience." See "Camus and the Theatre," in *The Cambridge Companion to Camus,* ed. Edward Hughes (Cambridge: Cambridge University Press, 2007), 71.

50. See Camus' preface to *Caligula and Three Other Plays,* trans. Stuart Gilbert (New York: Vintage, 1958).

51. Ibid., 245.

52. Ibid., 254.

53. Ibid., 256, 258.

54. Quoted in Foley, *Albert Camus: From the Absurd to Revolt*, 217.

55. I am indebted to John Foley's analysis in his article "Albert Camus and Political Violence," in *Albert Camus in the 21st Century*, ed. Christine Margerrison, Mark Orme, and Lissa Lincoln (Amsterdam: Rodopi, 2008), 219.

56. Camus, *The Rebel*, 170.

57. Camus, *Oeuvres completes*, 3:375.

58. Albert Camus, *Lyrical and Critical Essays*, trans. Ellen Kennedy (New York: Knopf, 1968), 148–149.

59. Thucydides, *The History of the Peloponnesian War*, 147.

60. Camus, *The Rebel*, 101.

61. Ibid., 13.

62. Ibid., 16.

63. Ibid., 22.

64. Ibid., 16.

65. Ibid., 289–290.

66. Camus, *Notebooks 1951–1959*, trans. Ryan Bloom (Chicago: Ivan Dee, 2008), 102.

67. Quoted in Alastair Horne, *A Savage War of Peace* (New York: Penguin, 1985), 132.

68. The bombing and its aftermath, as well as the French military's use of torture, are reenacted with meticulous and terrifying care in Gillo Pontecorvo's documentary *The Battle of Algiers*.

69. Camus, *Camus at Combat*, 200.

70. Albert Camus, *Oeuvres complètes*, vol. 4, ed. Raymond Gay-Crosier (Paris: Gallimard, 2008), 301.

71. Ibid., 299.

72. David Carroll, *Albert Camus the Algerian: Colonialism, Terrorism, Justice* (New York: Columbia University Press, 2007), 109. Carroll's sharp and astute book has helped shape my own understanding of Camus' attitude toward the FLN.

73. Camus, *Oeuvres complètes*, 4:300.

EPILOGUE

1. Albert Camus, *Oeuvres complètes,* vol. 4, ed. Raymond Gay-Crosier (Paris: Gallimard, 2008), 661.

2. Quoted in Ronald Aronson, *Camus and Sartre: The Story of a Friendship and the Quarrel that Ended It* (Chicago: University of Chicago Press, 2004), 147.

3. Albert Camus, *Notebooks, 1951–1959,* trans. Ryan Bloom (Chicago: Ivan Dee, 2008), 72.

4. Herbert Lottman, *Albert Camus* (Madera, CA: Gingko Press, 1997), 606.

5. Albert Camus, *Lyrical and Critical Essays,* trans. Ellen Kennedy (New York: Knopf, 1968), 167–168.

6. Ibid., 168–169.

7. *The Orwell Reader,* ed. Richard Rovere (New York: Harcourt, Brace, Jovanovich, 1956), 386.

8. Camus, *Oeuvres complètes,* 4:603.

9. Camus, *Notebooks, 1951–1959,* 73.

10. Camus, *Lyrical and Critical Essays,* 67.

11. Ibid., 165.

12. Quoted in Elaine Scarry, *On Beauty and Being Just* (Princeton: Princeton University Press, 1999), 94.

13. Ibid., 97.

14. *Simone Weil: An Anthology,* ed. Sian Reynolds (New York: Atheneum, 1986), 6.

15. Camus, *Lyrical and Critical Essays,* 37.

16. Ibid., 69. The photograph is reproduced in Catherine Camus, ed., *Albert Camus: Solitaire et Solidaire* (Paris: Lafon, 2009), 202.

17. Albert Camus, *The First Man,* trans. David Hapgood (New York: Knopf, 1994), 243.

ACKNOWLEDGMENTS

I could not have written this small book without the support of friends and colleagues. At Harvard University Press, my editor, John Kulka, encouraged me to take on the project— one I would not have carried to its end were it not for his sharp, yet always generous, criticism. At times we differed on elements to Camus' thought, but these differences were always based on our common conviction that Camus matters for our age. His editorial assistant, Heather Hughes, was unfailingly attentive and helpful, while Edward Wade oversaw a precise and punctual editing process. And I am very grateful for the many smart questions and encouraging words offered by the manuscript's two anonymous readers.

Closer to home, I need to thank Mallory Chesser and Paul Slavin for reading earlier chapters of the book. The dean of the Honors College, Bill Monroe, was unstinting in his support and encouragement. I also must thank my former professor Patrick Hutton, who invited me to write an article on Camus' tragic sense of nostalgia for a special issue of *Historical*

Reflections/Réflexions historiques. Pat's critical remarks helped me reconsider and reframe some of this book's themes. And I can never thank David Mikics enough for all he did to make this a better book than it otherwise would have been. Despite his own many professional and personal commitments, David read and reread the entire manuscript with his remarkable mix of unsparing criticism and unflagging enthusiasm.

Finally, there is home. My wife, Julie, and children, Ruben and Louisa, put up with a great deal over the last year and a half. And yet, they always gave me the time and love my book needed. For this, I will always be thankful.

It is to my teacher Douglas Hall that I wish to dedicate this book. When I walked into his class on the history of Christianity at McGill University, I encountered a professor who, with great humanity and intensity, drew us into a common search for meaning in our lives. Nearly forty years after this first encounter, he still reminds me what we should expect of ourselves as teachers as well as writers.

INDEX